UNLESS WE PRAY

THE HOUR IS LATE.
GOD HAS A PLAN AND THIS IS IT!

TODD SMITH

DESTINY IMAGE® PUBLISHERS, INC.

P.O. Box 310, Shippensburg, PA 17257-0310

"Promoting Inspired Lives."

This book and all other Destiny Image and Destiny Image Fiction books are available at Christian bookstores and distributors worldwide.

For more information on foreign distributors, call 717-532-3040.

Reach us on the Internet: www.destinyimage.com.

ISBN 13 TP: 978-0-7684-6485-6

ISBN 13 eBook: 978-0-7684-6486-3

ISBN 13 HC: 978-0-7684-6488-7

ISBN 13 LP: 978-0-7684-6487-0

For Worldwide Distribution, Printed in the U.S.A.

5 6 7 8 / 26 25 24 23

DEDICATION

I dedicate this book to the hundreds of faithful men, women, teenagers, and children who have continuously labored in prayer at Christ Fellowship Church, Dawsonville, Georgia. Your consistent intercession and contention for the face of God has created the perfect environment so people from all over the world can encounter the sweet and raw power of God. Together, our eyes have seen thousands of miracles, dramatic deliverances, and unspeakable life change in the baptismal waters of the North Georgia Revival. You have truly prayed the price.

After the revival started, the Lord's voice spoke to me. He said, "Revival sits on the shoulders of men." In other words, men and women get to determine the depth and magnitude of His manifest presence within a church and a revival. Christ Fellowship Church, you have faithfully and honorably carried the "revival" and the increasing weight of God's Glory.

Well done!

CONTENTS

LIONS ARE COMING FORTH

The mayhem and chaos in our culture is not slowing down. The uninvited guests of perversion, wickedness, hopelessness, confusion, and violence are here and kicking down doors with little to no resistance from both the physical and spiritual sides. Sadly, in these most trying times we the Church have grown eerily quiet and still.

The question begs to be asked, *"The Church, where is she?"* Where is the voice crying in the wilderness? Where is the bastion of life and peace? Where is that light on a hill? Where is the beam of hope—the lighthouse that weary sailors look for in troubled seas? Where is the flame of God that prepares the way of the Lord?

> *Where is the flame of God that prepares the way of the Lord?*

Honestly, by and large we retreated. We have hidden ourselves; we have withdrawn and linked arms with meekness and silence. We have been intimidated by the "woke" spirit that demands we conform to social norms. Furthermore, that same spirit dares us to speak up. Sadly, due to fear we have tucked ourselves away with a desperate and optimistic hope that things will somehow get better. We ponder, "Perhaps this nightmare will suddenly vanish and things will get back to normal."

I was once told by a very wise man that hope is not a strategy. Hoping is not enough. I am convinced things will never be normal again. This is the new current reality. A rugged frontier, a battlefield, and things are now different. Moving forward looks different than it did ten years ago. We have to come out of hiding—we have no choice. We must risk it all in order to make a difference in our society. The solitude and silence has to be broken. The great Oswald Chambers said, "The frontiers of the Kingdom of God were never advanced by men and women of caution."

In the midst of all the uncertainty, a deep yearning is emerging within the body of Christ. A holy anguish is surfacing, and people are ready for spiritual war. I see it everywhere I go. For far too long, the devil has dealt with docile, compliant, comfort-seeking sheep, but now he must prepare himself to deal with lions. There is fierceness entering the Church of the Lord Jesus, the like of which the devil hasn't witnessed since the book of Acts. This is one thing I know for certain—the hungry, longing, and desperate people of the Kingdom are adjusting, restructuring their lives for this moment. I am moved by the instruction the warrior Atticus gave to his soldiers: "Keep your head up; you are a lion. Don't forget that, and neither will the sheep."

> There is fierceness entering the Church of the Lord Jesus, the like of which the devil hasn't witnessed since the book of Acts.

The Lamb of God is arranging His warring army. The Bride, the Church, is and will continue to emerge and fall into ranks, and she will be different from what she has been. *The lions are being released!*

Hell is about to feel the fury of millions of praying lions—full of power, glory, and fire. This is a new era, a new season.

|| SECTION 1 ||

UNLESS WE DIE

|| 1 ||

DIE WELL

If you have not discovered something you are willing to die for, then you are not fit to live.
—MARTIN LUTHER KING, JR.

Jim Elliot was one of the five faithful missionaries who were killed with spears by the Auca Indians on January 8, 1956. He was attempting to evangelize the Huaorani people of Ecuador when they fatally attacked him and the others.

Several months after Jim's funeral, a friend of the family approached his widow, Elisabeth, and asked, "How do you deal with Jim's death, the fact that he was brutally killed with a spear that day in the jungle? Where he died, the way he died, how do you handle that?"

Elisabeth looked the friend straight in the eye and without hesitation she said, "My Jim didn't die in the jungle that day; my Jim died one night in high school while he knelt by his bed in agonizing, travailing prayer when he prayed this prayer: 'Lord Jesus, if You did all that You did for me that is written in that blessed holy book, then there is nothing I can do for You that will ever repay the debt I owe, so I commit myself here and now to go and do whatever You want me to do. I am Yours, do with me as You please.'" Then Elisabeth paused and said, "That's when my Jim died."

Tens of thousands of people have met the Lord in the baptismal waters at the North Georgia Revival. We have witnessed every kind of miracle imaginable and watched people have dramatic encounters with the Lord in the waters. People want to know what I share with the candidates before they are baptized. My words are simple and the same every time, "*Die well.*" Typically, I get a subtle smile and a nervous laugh, as if to indicate to me, "Are you joking? What do you mean?" And when my expression doesn't change they realize I am serious, and the severity of the moment sinks into their heart. You see, according to Romans 6 baptism is likened unto a burial, a death. I know it sounds a little morbid, but it is the best advice I could give them.

I tell people all the time that the degree to which you are willing to die to yourself will determine the degree to which God will use you. The depth of my repentance and brokenness determines how effective I am for the Kingdom of God. I wholeheartedly believe you and I get to choose to what level God uses us. God places that decision in your hands. A.W. Tozer said, "Every man is as full of the Holy Spirit as he wants to be. He may or may not be as full as he wishes he were, but he is most certainly as full as he wants to be." Again, we get to choose.

> The degree to which you are willing to die to yourself will determine the degree to which God will use you.

The wonderful Kathryn Kuhlman, while addressing a massive crowd of young people, said, "God has not given to me one thing that He will not give to any one of you young people in this place if you will pay the price. …God will use you exactly the same way. He will give to you absolutely everything He has given to me if you will pay the price." She added, "I would lie if I were to tell you the price is cheap. Everybody is out for a bargain these days, but God has no bargains."[1] Then in another miracle crusade she said these infamous words that marked the power of her ministry. "Kathryn Kuhlman died a long time ago. I know the day, I know the hour, I can go to the spot where Kathryn Kuhlman died."

History has been kind to reveal to us there are certain criteria God looks for when He sets out to use a person greatly. Not every variable is identical, but there are certain distinctives that are present in each. It requires complete surrender, abandonment, isolation, sacrifice, and giving oneself to prayer. Obviously, this list is not exhaustive, but these variables were present in each and are non-negotiable for us today. Because the price is high for this realm of expression of Holy Spirit power, it remains unrealized by the vast majority of believers. However, once this pathway is fully embraced one is ushered into a place of heavenly strength, power, and peace that confounds the natural mind. Again, and sadly, because of its price many do not walk along its path.

T.M. Anderson spoke a warning to leaders who do not choose this path; he said, "The results of his neglect of prayer will be revealed by the poverty of his preaching. It is possible for a minister to become so preoccupied with his duties that he will give prayer a place of secondary importance in his life. God's servants should consider that nothing pertaining to the church of Christ is more important than waiting before the Lord in the secret place of prayer."[2]

R.A. Torrey lamented the constant busyness of today's pastors and Christians, who at times seem powerless. Torrey said, "We are too busy to pray, and so we are too busy to have power. We have a great deal of activity, but we accomplish little; many services but few conversions; much machinery but few results."

In David Brainerd's journal June 29, 1746, these words were found, "Oh, for spirituality and holy fervency that I might spend and be spent for God to my latest moment!"[3] This is the heart posture we need in this desperate hour.

It was Hudson Taylor, the great missionary to China, who said, "God isn't looking for people of great faith, but for individuals ready to follow Him." And then he added,

"When God wants to do His great works, He trains somebody to be quiet enough and little enough, then He uses that person."

My prayer is that this book will prepare you to be quiet and little enough to be used by God.

Die well!

TWO PRAYERS THAT CHANGED THE WORLD

*I'd rather hear my father pray
than anybody in the world.*

—BILLY GRAHAM

Before his death at the age of 99, Billy Graham had set foot in 185 countries and preached the gospel to more people in live audiences than anyone else in history. His first official crusade was in 1947 in Grand Rapids, Michigan, and his last evangelistic outreach was in 2005 in New York City, in a packed Madison Square Garden. Between those two dates, the Billy Graham Evangelistic Association claims that 3.2 million people became born again as a result of his preaching. They estimate that he reached a total audience of 2.2 billion through radio and television, books, and events. In 58 years of public ministry, he led over 400 indoor and outdoor crusades across the world.[1] During his ministry he endeared himself to the American public and became known as "America's pastor."

Growing up, I remember watching Dr. Graham preach the gospel on television. I was mesmerized by the size of the crowds. He packed the largest stadiums in the world as people came by the tens of thousands to hear the good news proclaimed from this tall but fiery evangelist from a dairy farm in Charlotte, North Carolina.

IT ALL STARTED IN A BARN

Before Billy Graham was saved, Graham's father, William Franklin Graham, Sr., joined a group of businessmen who had a burden due to the spiritual condition of the world. They faithfully gathered in the Graham's barn to pray for Charlotte and the unsaved around the globe.

One day a few local businessmen along with his father came together for prayer in the barn. In another part of the barn, Billy was attending to his daily chores. At the time, Billy was an unsaved 15-year-old teenager. One of the men, Vernon Patterson, a paper salesman, encouraged the group to pray a bold prayer: "that God would raise up someone from Charlotte, North Carolina, who would take the Gospel to the ends of the earth."[2] Billy Graham listened to that prayer and later wrote about what he heard, "It certainly wasn't obvious that that someone might be me."

Within six months, a reluctant teenager attended an evangelistic meeting conducted by Mordecai Ham. He went to the meeting because he was curious and wanted to know what was happening in the services. He came to observe all of the activity, and on November 1, 1934, six days after his 16th birthday, Graham was dramatically born again. Underneath that revival tent, the prayers of those businessmen were answered. A sixteen-year-old Graham would be commissioned by God as an "Evangelist to the World" and a "Pastor to Presidents." His son, Franklin, said, "God answered that prayer in ways beyond anything anyone could have imagined."[3]

We must not lose sight of the fact that our prayers matter. I am convinced that if these men had not prayed the prayer they prayed, the world would have never encountered the ministry of Billy Graham. Their faith and obedience released an international harvester of souls. Jesus encourages us to pray the exact same way those businessmen prayed.

The harvest truly is great, but the laborers are few; therefore pray the Lord of the harvest to send out laborers into His harvest (Luke 10:2 NKJV).

> **We must not lose sight of the fact that our prayers matter.**

Prayer Number 2

In 1940, six years after his conversion at the age of 22, while on a college ministry tour, students under the oversight of Dr. J. Edwin Orr visited sites of great revivals. They came to Epworth rectory where the students had the privilege to enter a historical place—John Wesley's bedroom. Wesley, the famous reformer, received national and international attention because he led the way for a substantial spiritual renewal in America during the 1700s. In addition, he founded the Methodist movement.

After they entered the room, Dr. Orr showed the inquisitive students two worn impressions in the carpet where it was said that John Wesley knelt for hours in prayer, crying out for revival to sweep through his beloved England and across the Atlantic to America. Each student was touched by what they saw and felt; however, one of them had a much different heart cry and encounter.

After their brief stay in the bedroom, the students were instructed to get on the bus. As the students were getting on the bus, Dr. Orr noticed one of his students was missing. Methodically retracing his steps, Dr. Orr went back upstairs to Wesley's bedroom, and as he entered he found Graham with his face on the bed and kneeling in the same worn-out carpet holes. Where Wesley fervently prayed for revival, Graham repeatedly prayed to God, "*Oh Lord, do it again! Do it again! And would You do it again with me?*"

Dr. Orr leaned forward and placed a hand on Graham's shoulder and said gently, "Come on, Billy, we must be going." And rising from the ground he was forever changed—God heard and answered the desperate cry, "*Oh Lord, do it again! Do it again!*" And God did!

In 1949, nine years after his prayer in Wesley's bedroom, God answered his prayer. Graham had scheduled a three-week tent meeting in the heart of Los Angeles. The evangelistic crusade was a huge success and lasted eight weeks. Billy Graham's ministry impacted the entire city. The Holy Spirit moved in a profound way as many souls fell under deep conviction and were saved. This crusade launched Graham onto the national scene.[4]

God did it again!

Lest we forget it was John Wesley who declared:

> Give me one hundred preachers who fear nothing but sin, and desire nothing but God, and I care not a straw whether they be clergymen or laymen; such alone will shake the gates of hell and set up the kingdom of heaven on earth.

Can you imagine what would happen if people prayed the exact prayer that Billy Graham prayed?

He would do it again!

In short order the world would be engulfed in revival fire.

3

THE STRONG MAN HAS BEEN BOUND!

Do not have your concert first, and tune your instruments afterward. Begin the day with God.
—J. HUDSON TAYLOR

I came across a story that accurately describes satan's strategy when it comes to prayer.

Satan called a worldwide convention. In his opening address to his throng of demons, he said, "We can't keep the Christians from going to church. We can't keep them from worshiping God and reading their Bibles. We can't even keep them from being good. But we can do something else. We can keep them from tapping into the power of prayer. Yes, that is our goal, to keep them from the one thing that is the greatest threat to our world dominance. I commission you to make this your highest aim—keep the church from praying!"

He continued, "If they realize what they can accomplish in prayer, then we will lose this war. So let them go to church, let them have their Christian lifestyles, but minimize this discipline. Steal their time, their energy, their hunger so they will not gather together in prayer. At all costs this is what I want you to do. Distract them from gaining hold of prayer."

"How shall we do this?" asked his demons.

"Keep them busy with the nonessentials of life. Unleash an assault of things to occupy their minds," he answered. "Tempt them to spend, spend, spend, then borrow, borrow, borrow. Convince them to work six or seven days a week, ten to twelve hours a day, so they can afford their lifestyles. Keep them from spending time with their children. As their families fragment, soon their homes will offer no escape from the pressures of work. Overstimulate their minds, cause them to be addicted to frivolous things, things that add little to no value to their walk with God. Entice them to watch YouTube, Netflix, and listen to meaningless podcasts. Have them fixated with social media so they spend hours scanning, reading, and responding to posts. Keep them and their children enamored with video games. Also, keep them occupied with information and more information."

He added, "Even in their recreation, let them be excessive. Have them make family their highest of all priorities. Have them return from their holidays exhausted, disquieted, and disengaged. Make their personal happiness their supreme objective. Condemn them from past mistakes so they feel ineffective and unworthy to pray with others. Also, my favorite, highlight all their failures in prayer—you know, the things they prayed for that never got answered."

He added, "Let them be involved in evangelism; without prayer they will lack power. But crowd their lives with so many good causes that they have no time to pray to seek power from Christ. Soon they will be working in their own strength, sacrificing their health and family unity for the good of the cause. Above all things, sacrifice whatever you need to in order to minimize the priority of prayer. At all costs," he shouted, "keep them from prayer!"

Every demon jumped to their feet and hailed the new assignment. It was quite a convention. And the demons eagerly sped to their assignments and did exactly as instructed.

Has the devil been successful in his scheme? You be the judge.[1]

I am strongly convinced the devil is doing everything that is mentioned above!

WHAT COLOR WERE MARY'S EYES?

It was reported that the city of Constantinople, which fell to the Turks in 1495, was being attacked. Inside the city, the Christian monks were busy discussing trivial things like debating the sex of angels, the color of the eyes of the Virgin Mary, and, "If a fly should fall into holy water, would the fly be sanctified or the water polluted?" While they gave themselves to non-essential issues and meaningless religious discussions, their city methodically and tragically fell to Muslims.

If we are not careful, the Church will make the same mistake the monks made—engrossed in our own issues, debating trivial concerns, and becoming stagnated in nonsensical arguments. Therefore, we become disconnected from the real state of affairs and even unaware of the subtle but deadly advancement of the enemy. The Bible warns us of this: *"that we would not be outwitted by Satan; for we are not ignorant of his designs"* (2 Corinthians 2:11 ESV).

The devil is our chief adversary and the Bible instructs us to, *"Be sober, be vigilant; because your adversary the devil walks about like a roaring lion, seeking whom he may devour"* (1 Peter 5:8 NKJV). Furthermore, in Ephesians 2:2 satan is called the *"prince of the power of the air"* and it says that spirit is at work among us in the sons of disobedience.

Don't miss the announcement that said satan *is at work among us.* Wow! Most people probably don't believe this; however, if it is true, and it is, we must be alert and active in confronting, minimizing, and neutralizing his activity.

TAKE OUT THE STRONG MAN!

Jesus gave a fascinating illustration regarding spiritual warfare. *"When a strong man, fully armed, guards his own house, his possessions are safe. But when someone stronger attacks and overpowers him, he takes away the armor in which the man trusted and divides up his plunder"* (Luke 11:21-22 NIV). Mark 3:27 (NKJV) says it this way:

> *No one can enter a strong man's house and plunder his goods, unless he first binds the strong man.*

The teaching of Jesus in this passage is revealing. He states when you want to overtake a person and their valuables, the first order is to neutralize the strongest threat. The strongman has to be put out of commission in order to plunder the goods within a house. When you dispose the threat, then you can exert your will against anything that opposes you. Once the strongman is tied up, the rest is easy.

The exercise of neutralizing the strongman works in the Kingdom of God and the kingdom of satan. In my opinion, the strongman of the Church is *prayer*. The devil knows if he is to accomplish his goals, he has to eliminate the greatest threat—the very thing that could cause his goals to not be achieved. So, he tenderly walks into a church and ever so gently binds the strongman. And in this case it isn't a person but a weapons system a church uses to advance the cause of Christ—*prayer*. He ties it up! His strategy is cunning and subtle, but quite effective. What makes this so startling is oftentimes the strongman of prayer has been bound and very few people, if anybody, know it.

I think it has become clear over the years that the devil has been successful in minimizing the emphasis of prayer in our churches. One way he does this is he encourages leadership to delegate the ministry of prayer to a few special people within the Church—the ones called to pray, "the intercessors." Here is an example I recently heard about. A seasoned pastor who was being interviewed by another church for the lead pastor position was asked for his view on prayer and the role it plays in his life and the church. Obviously, he quickly responded by saying he believed in the power of prayer and its necessity. However, he added, it wasn't his strength and he wasn't called to it. He added that he would leave the ministry of prayer to the "intercessors" within the church.

As sad as this is, it has become far too familiar. The responsibility of prayer has been given over to a select few "prayer warriors" in the church. This mindset is prevalent and must be changed.

Let me be as emphatic as I can at this point. Prayer cannot be viewed as "a ministry of the church" like the youth ministry or children's ministry; it has to be *the* ministry of the church. It must be elevated above everything else the church does. Hear my heart—I am thankful for all the intercessors in our churches, but they cannot carry the entire load. Without their dedication, the church would be worse off than she is already. The responsibility of prayer belongs first to the lead pastor, the elders, and the staff of the church and then the whole church. The prayer emphasis of the church must not be left for a few select "prayer warriors" who feel "called by God" to pray. Also, you can't address the great needs of our time to a loosely connected "prayer chain" ministry.

> **Prayer has to be the ministry of the church.**

PREACHING AND WORSHIP ARE GREAT BUT NOT ENOUGH

Have you ever noticed in our churches we always have preaching and worship? These two are of utmost importance to the Church and should never be discarded. Assuredly, the devil doesn't like these Kingdom expressions, but he also knows these alone are not what threaten his dominance. The devil is after the prayer arm of the Church; it is what threatens him the most.

Let me be as clear as I can. I am under the persuasion that nothing a church does is more important than prayer—absolutely nothing. I know this is somewhat of a controversial proclamation, but it is the truth and can be validated both historically and biblically. I am not minimizing the other key expressions of our faith, but prayer is the foundation. Therefore, it is the fuel that makes the other ministry endeavors dynamic.

Tragically, we have allowed the devil to come into our churches and minimize prayer. Therefore, he has successfully bound the strongman of the Church, which is prayer. What has been the result? The enemy has walked into our house unopposed and successfully plundered our young people, our homes, our schools, our churches, our communities, and even our government. Hell and its agenda, for the most part, has been able to operate with little to no substantial opposition. There have been groups who have held the line to resist him, but he is killing, stealing, and destroying just like he said he would (see John 10:10).

Not to oversimplify, but the devil distracted us, shifted our focus off of prayer. We put our energy and efforts in other good places—we promoted programs, ministries, and presentations that would attract larger crowds to our buildings. Our goal was to get people in our seats and keep them returning to church. Again, this is not bad, but most, if not all, of our energy went to such endeavors. We maximized the good over the most important. We became busy, active, pursuing people and, I must say, somewhat successfully. But the sacrifice was that we underemphasized and therefore minimized personal and corporate prayer meetings.

Here is how the forces of hell try to keep us from praying:

- Minimizing the priority of prayer in the minds of leaders
- Speaking about it but not practicing it
- Persuading people to focus on the more tangible needs of the church
- God is control anyway; His will will always be done
- They can pray from home; people are too busy to come to the church and pray

I do believe the world is under the consequential sway of the evil one because the key component of prayer has been successfully minimized and bound by the devil. For multiple reasons, we have not faithfully implemented the one weapon the devil fears the most—prayer.

I think Guy H. King said it best, "No one is a firmer believer in the power of prayer than the devil; not that he practices it, but he suffers from it." This is why he fights it at every turn.

4

GOD IS LIMITED

*The only way to persevere in prayer
is to burn every other bridge.*
—Corey Russell, *Prayer: Why
Our Words to God Matter*

The most-practiced religious exercise around the world is prayer. Billions of people pray each day, each in their own language and to their particular deity or god. The thread of prayer is woven through every sect of society. Both rich and poor pray; the educated and uneducated alike pray. Christians and satanists pray. Those who live in multimillion-dollar mansions as well as the homeless pray. Addicts pray, and when things get bad enough even some atheists pray. We all pray. Prayer is a staple of human society.

God's Purpose for Prayer

Simply put, God set man on the earth to have dominion, to rule, and to subdue it. God chose to govern the world in cooperation and in fellowship with His children. Below are a few texts that reveal God's heart regarding His relationship with man and the earth.

> *Then God said, "Let Us make man in Our image, according to Our likeness; let them have dominion over the fish of the sea, over the birds of the air, and over the cattle, over all the earth and over every creeping thing that creeps on the earth." So God created man in His own image; in the image of God He created him; male and female He created them. Then God blessed them, and God said to them, "Be fruitful and multiply; fill the earth and subdue it; have dominion over the fish of the sea, over the birds of the air, and over every living thing that moves on the earth"* (Genesis 1:26-28 NKJV).

What God said in these verses brings purpose and clarity to our role on the earth. God said, *"Let them have dominion… over all the earth"* (Genesis 1:26 NKJV). He added in verses 28, *"fill the earth and subdue it."* Notice God said, *"Let them"* and He did not say, "Let Us" have dominion and rule the earth, in reference to the Godhead. God gave that authority to us—man.

What does this mean? Man has authority on the earth—legal authority given to us by God to exercise dominion in the earth. In short, we are the overseers of planet Earth. Now, I understand God created it, owns it, and at any time could choose to destroy it if He wanted to; however, He has placed man in charge of it—we are managers of it. This is what He implied in Psalm 8:6 (CSB):

> *You made him ruler over the works of your hands;*
> *you put everything under his feet.*

And also, Psalm 115:16 (NKJV):

> *The heaven, even the heavens, are the Lord's; but*
> *the earth He has given to the children of men.*

Did it ever occur to you that in the beginning when God created mankind, He didn't create man to be an occupant of heaven? Also, did it cross your mind that when Adam and Eve first walked in the Garden, satan was not the "god" of this world (see 2 Corinthians 4:4)? According to the biblical account, when Adam succumbed to the temptation he surrendered and submitted rulership and dominion of the earth to satan and the kingdom of darkness. It was at that time satan stepped into his new authority and assumed the title *"god of this world"* (2 Corinthians 4:4). This new position was legally granted to him by Adam. Since that time, mankind and the entire earth has been draped in the spirit of darkness that permeates all of society, and satan's agenda saturates the world. Sadly, in most cases his influence goes uninhibited with little to no prevailing light to resist it.

According to the teachings of Jesus, the only ones who can stop the progression of evil are God's people. However, it just does not, nor will it, come easy; we have to stand in the position of authority and power. You see, God's original script for mankind is still intact; His purpose hasn't changed. He created man to inhabit and rule the earth. The difference now is we have to fight a spiritual war for everything due to the dark rulership over the planet.

> **Man was created for and assigned the legal authority on the earth.**

MAN IS LEGAL AUTHORITY

The point must be clearly made—man was created for and assigned the legal authority on the earth. Again, man was not brought into existence to have dominion in heaven but on the earth. God's commission was clear and straightforward—henceforth, the earth was and still is currently under man's management.

Let me state again, *God put man on earth to manage it*, yet God is still the owner of it all.

Let me give you an example of how this works in the natural. It is a given that no matter how incredible and awesome an owner is, the people they have working for them determine the success of the business or lack thereof.

The owner may be very conscientious, organized, a people person, a planner, very *skilled*, talented, and even have a wonderful, well-thought-out business plan. *But,* the manager they have hired who oversees the day-to-day activities may not be as conscientious as the owner—their heart may be good, but they may not pay attention to the details. They may be unorganized, lazy, scattered, and one who doesn't finish tasks in a timely manner. Therefore, the owner is left at the mercy of those who are assigned to operate their business.

God experienced this type of scenario. When He created Adam and Eve, they were responsible for conducting the Father's business on the earth. However, when they sinned things shifted.

Even to this day the powers of dark principalities and demonic hosts of wickedness propagate the will of their leader across the world. According to the Bible, the world is *under the sway* or *control* of the devil. This means that the world is also under the dominion and power of the devil. The Greek word for *sway* or *under control* is *keimai* and means "lies in the power of the evil one," i.e. is *held in subjection* by the devil.

Here are a few different translations of 1 John 5:19 that portray the imagery perfectly:

> *We know that we are of God, and the whole world lies under the sway of the wicked one* (1 John 5:19 NKJV).
>
> *We know that we are children of God and that the world around us is under the control of the evil one* (1 John 5:19 NLT).

We know that we are from God, and the whole world lies in the power of the evil one (1 John 5:19 ESV).

We are certain we come from God and the rest of the world is under the power of the devil (1 John 5:19 CEV).

If history has taught us anything, those who are in power can dictate and influence the direction, health, and culture of society, whether good or bad. Likewise, the earth moves in the direction of those who are in charge and in power.

Currently there are two competing powers—God and satan. Satan and his demons oversee the earth. He has it easy. All who are born are a part of his family. His nature is in every one of his descendants. He has to do nothing to recruit new members. However, God sees the sons and daughters of men and works from the time they are born to compel them to join His family—the family of God.

Let me add, man still has jurisdiction on the earth. For the most part, man gets to control what takes place in this time-space dimension. God's interaction and intervention in the world is largely based upon man's pursuit of Him and the prayers they pray. Please read these words carefully—I am not suggesting God is disconnected from the earth and doesn't intervene from time to time. He does, but God's involvement usually comes when someone prays in faith that the will of God be done. Once again, God's power engagement with the world is directly linked to the prayers of His people; He works in concert with them.

> God's power engagement with the world is directly linked to the prayers of His people; He works in concert with them.

When we pray, we are literally going before God and asking Him to intervene in the affairs of man—in our world. Here, perhaps, is one of the best explanations of prayer:

Prayer is man exercising his legal authority on earth to invoke heaven's influence on the planet.[1]

This is how Jesus taught His disciples. He instructed them to ask, "Father, Your Kingdom *come* on earth *as it is* in heaven" (see Matthew 6:10).

Here are a few other passages that strongly imply God's initial intent when He created us.

I will give you the keys (authority) of the kingdom of heaven; and whatever you bind [forbid, declare to be improper and unlawful] on earth will have [already] been bound in heaven, and whatever you loose [permit, declare lawful] on earth will have [already] been loosed in heaven (Matthew 16:19 AMP).

Truly I tell you, whatever you bind on earth will be bound in heaven, and whatever you loose on earth will be loosed in heaven. Again, truly I tell you that if two of you on earth agree about anything you ask for, it will be done for them by my Father in heaven. For where two or three gather in my name, there am I with them (Matthew 18:18-20 NIV).

In short, God lovingly invites us into His government and oversight of the world. Our prayers matter and, greater still, how we pray matters. In fact, when we don't pray or stop praying altogether we are actually inhibiting God's purposes from coming to pass on the earth. And the negative result is that satan's kingdom gains more influence.

John Wesley, who founded the Methodist movement along with his brother Charles, once said, "God does nothing but in answer to prayer."[2]

I know that is a bodacious statement, and if we are completely honest we don't like it because it just doesn't seem accurate or even believable.

Why does this bother us so much?

At first glance it seems to indicate that the omnipotent God we have grown to love can somehow be limited and hindered from doing what He wants to do.

Is that even possible?

What do you think?

According to the Bible, God can be limited. Israel did it, and so can we:

Yes, again and again they tempted God, and limited the Holy One of Israel (Psalm 78:41 NKJV).

What does all of this mean? I think it is simple, but at the same time troubling. Let me explain. Simple because if we don't take prayer seriously and learn how to pray correctly God is actually limited in what He does and can do on the earth. Troubling because it puts the responsibility squarely on our shoulders to bring, activate, and release the Kingdom of heaven to the earth. Indirectly, we are responsible for how much of heaven touches the earth. And if we don't pray and implore God to interact and intervene with humanity, things on the earth follow their natural course, which we all know is exactly what the devil wants.

> **We are responsible for how much of heaven touches the earth.**

Watchman Nee made a startling yet true statement:

> Many matters are piled up in heaven, many transactions remain undone, simply because God is unable to find an outlet for His will on the earth. The manifestation of God's power may not exceed the prayer of the church. …In heaven God's power is unlimited, but on earth today the manifestation of His power is dependent on how much the church prays.[3]

The question needs to be asked, "How can we utilize prayer to touch heaven in order to bring the Kingdom of God to the earth?"

|| 5 ||

YOUR VOICE MATTERS

*The angel fetched Peter out of prison, but
it was prayer that fetched the angel.*
—THOMAS WATSON

One of the mightiest men of prayer of the 19th century was George Mueller of Bristol, England (1805–1898). He cared for over 10,000 orphans during his lifetime. He also coordinated and established 117 schools, which offered Christian education to more than 120,000, of which most were poor. He was considered by many to be a leading authority on prayer. Before he died, he had listed in his journals over 50,000 answers to prayer, 30,000 of which he said were answered the same day and some the very same hour that he prayed.

R.A. Torey made this observation about Mueller's prayer life:

George Mueller never prayed for a thing just because he wanted it, or even just because he felt it was greatly needed for God's work. When it was laid upon George Mueller's heart to pray for anything, he would search the Scriptures to find if there was some promise that covered the case. Sometimes he would search the scriptures for days before he presented his petition to God. And then when he found the promise, with his open Bible before him, and his finger upon that promise, he would plead that promise, and so he received what he asked. He always prayed with an open Bible before him.[1]

Mueller lived and manifested the goodness of 1 John 5:14-15 (NKJV):

> *Now this is the confidence that we have in Him, that if we ask anything according to His will, He hears us. And if we know that He hears us, whatever we ask, we know that we have the petitions that we have asked of Him.*

Here are a few of the many principles he applied when he went to the Lord in prayer.

- "I get my heart into such a state that it has no will of its own in regard to any particular matter."

- "I seek God's will through, or in connection with His Word. If you look to the Spirit without the Word, you open yourself to delusion."
- "I ask God in prayer to reveal His will to me."
- "I make sure I have a clear conscience before God and man."
- "I act only when I am at peace, after much prayer, waiting on God with faith."[2]

He was thoroughly convinced that God loved him and wanted him to pray: "I always firmly believed in the willingness of God to hear my prayers" (see Mark 11:24).

He also added, "Every time I listened to men instead of God, I made serious mistakes."

DON'T UNDERESTIMATE WHAT YOU PRAY

I have discovered the impact of prayer is universal, especially when you pray in tongues. What do I mean? When you pray in the Spirit, you are praying the perfect will of God; therefore, you affect the heavenly realm, and in return the heavenly realm is released to implement the will of the Kingdom of God on the earth. Here are a couple of Kingdom truths:

1. God wants you to pray to Him.

2. God listens for your voice—yes, He does, and not because He has to but because He longs to hear from you.

David was so overwhelmed with God's willingness to hear from His servant that he wrote:

> *I love the Lord, because He has heard my voice and my supplications. Because He has inclined His ear to me, therefore I will call upon Him as long as I live* (Psalm 116:1-2 NKJV).

The Hebrew word for *incline* is *nāṭâ*, which means "the Lord turns and bends down to hear." God is not distant from us and He doesn't take the posture of being disinterested in our whispers of desperation or praise to Him. The great news is that God is ready to answer and show forth His power on your behalf.

> **God is ready to answer and show forth His power on your behalf.**

Let these scriptures build your faith!

> *Call to Me, and I will answer you, and show you great and mighty things, which you do not know* (Jeremiah 33:3 NKJV).
>
> *It shall come to pass that before they call, I will answer; and while they are still speaking, I will hear* (Isaiah 65:24 NKJV).
>
> *This poor man cried out, and the Lord heard him, and saved him out of all his troubles. …The eyes of the Lord are on the righteous, and His ears are open*

to their cry. The face of the Lord is against those who do evil, to cut off the remembrance of them from the earth. The righteous cry out, and the Lord hears, and delivers them out of all their troubles (Psalm 34:6,15-17 NKJV).

How precious also are Your thoughts to me, O God! How great is the sum of them! (Psalm 139:17 NKJV)

Now this is the confidence that we have in Him, that if we ask anything according to His will, He hears us. And if we know that He hears us, whatever we ask, we know that we have the petitions that we have asked of Him (1 John 5:14-15 NKJV).

The Lord hears us! His ears are *open!* Think about it—over 7.5 billion people occupy the earth, and in the midst of all the chaos that is happening on the planet God knows my distinct voice and lovingly and longingly desires to hear it. This alone is a standing invitation to bring our petitions before Him.

The magnitude of your prayers under no circumstance should ever be minimized, and any attempt to do so is of the devil. Furthermore, let me encourage you, you are not a burden to the Lord. You are His child and He will respond to you. Don't let the devil twist the truth of those statements. The devil is a liar and cannot speak the truth. Your voice matters to the Lord. I need you to understand that you have a role to play. Let this scripture encourage you:

Let us therefore come boldly to the throne of grace,
that we may obtain mercy and find grace to help in
time of need (Hebrews 4:16 NKJV).

You are not a burden to the Lord. You are His child and He will respond to you.

Pastor H.B. Charles of Shiloh Metropolitan Church, Jacksonville, Florida, told the following story in a sermon that illustrates the point I am trying to make:

My pastor was here a week ago and he told me about a woman in church. Every week she prayed the same prayer: "O Lord, thank You, Jesus." Every week that was her prayer. "O Lord, thank You, Jesus." Kids laughed because they knew what she was going to pray every time: "O Lord, thank You, Jesus." Finally somebody asked her, "Why do you pray the same little prayer?" She said, "Well, I'm just combining the two prayers that I know." She says, "We live in a bad neighborhood, and some nights there are bullets flying and I have to grab my daughter and hide on the floor, and in that desperate state all I know how to cry out is, 'O Lord.' But when I wake up in the morning and see that we're okay I say, 'Thank You, Jesus.' When I get to take my baby to the bus stop and she gets on that bus and

I don't know what's going to happen to her while she's away, I cry, 'O Lord.' And then when 3:00 p.m. comes and that bus arrives and my baby is safe, I say, 'Thank You, Jesus.'" She said, "Those are the only two prayers I know, and when I get to church God has been so good I just put my two prayers together, 'O Lord, thank You, Jesus!'"

God Is Waiting

Imagine what condition this world would be in if it were not for intercessors all over the world. Darkness would cover the earth and suffocate men into bondage and eternal damnation. Thankfully, there are some who pray; their prayers are a defeating force against the devil and his minions. Whenever the gospel goes forth and a harvest is gathered, it is because someone or some group cleared the way. E.M. Bounds stated, "God's vengeance is stayed by prayer, and God's penalty is remitted by prayer. The whole range of God's dealing with man is affected by prayer."[3] In essence, our prayers bring an intervention from God.

Take a close look at various translations of James 5:16 and see how important your prayer life is and what God will do when you pray.

> *The heartfelt and persistent prayer of a righteous man (believer) can accomplish much [when put into action and made effective by God—it is dynamic and can have tremendous power]* (AMP).

The prayer of a righteous person is powerful and effective (NIV).

The earnest prayer of a righteous person has great power and produces wonderful results (NLT).

The effective, fervent prayer of a righteous man avails much (NKJV).

The urgent request of a righteous person is very powerful in its effect (Holman Christian Standard Bible).

Whatever you do, you cannot remain silent. You can no longer assume God's will will be done in situations that concern you, your loved ones, and the Kingdom of God. Your involvement is a must. Many things on the earth that are God's will are not being set into motion or accomplished due to the lack of engagement from His people—this includes prayer.

> **Whatever you do, you cannot remain silent.**

Right now, tell the Lord that you are making yourself available to pray. Okay, starting right now be obedient to every nudge to pray by the Holy Spirit. This will happen—you will feel a tug on your heart or an uneasiness in your spirit. When this happens, the Lord is calling you to pray. The Lord needs you to release the will of God through intercession. Sometimes these promptings of the Spirit to pray come at unusual and uncomfortable times. It could be at dinner with your family or a gathering of friends—surrender to it nonetheless. The Lord is looking to you to activate the will of God in a particular situation and the issue needs your immediate attention. These moments are time sensitive, so obey and yield to the call to pray promptly. In fact, someone's life could be at stake, or a missionary needs prayer covering to be kept from harm, or a family member may be undergoing a temptation and your prayers aid their victory. Don't treat those moments lightly; make yourself available to pray when God needs you.

Your voice matters!

|| 6 ||

UNCOMMON POWER!

*Can demons remain in your presence? You
have to be greater than demons. Can disease lodge in the body that you touch? You
have to be greater than the disease.*
—SMITH WIGGLESWORTH,
"Faith in the Living Word"

J esus was in an undisclosed place of prayer, and when He
finished praying His disciples asked Him to teach them
to pray like He prayed. It is interesting to note the disciples
did not ask Him how to perform miracles, raise the dead, or
to teach or even preach like Him, but they wanted to learn
how to pray like He prayed.

Andrew Murray explains in his book *With Christ in the
School of Prayer*:

> The disciples had been with Christ and had
> seen Him pray. They had learned to understand

something of the connection between His wondrous life in public, and His secret life of prayer. They had learned to believe in Him as a Master in the art of prayer. None could pray like Him. And so they went to Him with the request, "Lord, teach us to pray."[1]

If we are not careful we can approach prayer with the wrong motives and purpose. We cannot overstate the truth that prayer is not simply an exercise for us to coerce God into doing what we want, nor is it forcing my desires or wishes on God and demanding He do it. Effective prayer is learning what the will of God is and praying from that perspective. The focus must be His will and nothing more. We can no longer afford to have biased or tainted prayer efforts—it is a waste of time.

According to the biblical narrative, it is seen that Jesus prioritized prayer in His life. Here are a few verses that highlight His prayer life.

After he had dismissed them, he went up on a mountainside by himself to pray (Matthew 14:23 NIV).

Then Jesus went with his disciples to a place called Gethsemane, and he said to them, "Sit here while I go over there and pray" (Matthew 26:36 NIV).

Very early in the morning, while it was still dark, Jesus got up, left the house and went off to a solitary place, where he prayed (Mark 1:35 NIV).

But Jesus often withdrew to lonely places and prayed (Luke 5:16 NIV).

One of those days Jesus went out to a mountainside to pray, and spent the night praying to God (Luke 6:12 NIV).

The result of Jesus' prayer was felt by all who were with Him. Every time Jesus prayed, He saw results.

The more we pray and seek God, the more of His power comes upon us.

FACTORIES NO LONGER FUNCTIONAL

While in Utica, New York, Charles Finney was asked by the owner to come to his cotton mill. As Finney walked in, a young lady employee who opposed Finney's meetings saw him. Glancing at another employee, she began to laugh. Some accounts say she made a cynical remark. Charles Finney simply looked at this young lady in a spirit of prayer, without saying a word. He kept looking at her, grieved by her criticism. Then, the lady broke her thread and had to stop working. She couldn't seem to repair the thread and start again, and she became upset. The Spirit of God began to mightily convict her of her sin, and she began to weep. Soon her coworkers were convicted and also began to weep. In a chain reaction, hundreds began to be overcome by their lost condition.

The owner of the factory, who was deeply moved himself, said, "Stop the mill, and let the people attend to religion, for it is far more important that our souls be saved than the factory run." The workers all assembled in a very large room, and Finney later said, "A more powerful meeting I scarcely ever attended." Within a few days, nearly every one of the 3,000 employees in the factory were saved.[2]

Why did this occur? Finney was given to prayer.

> **The more we pray and seek God, the more of His power comes upon us.**

You Convict Me!

There is a well-known story about Smith Wigglesworth while he was riding in a passenger train. The train stopped and picked up new passengers. Two men boarded the train and took their seats close to Smith. Smith was minding his own business when one man said, "Sir, you convict us of our sins. What must we do to be saved?"

On a separate occasion, again while Smith was traveling by train, a man walked near where he was sitting, looked at Smith, and cried out, "You convict me of sin!" He then ran out of the car. Without saying a word, the power of the Holy Ghost convicted that man of sin.

Smith refused to contaminate himself with the things of the world. He said, "If I read the newspaper I come out dirtier than I went in. If I read my Bible, I come out cleaner than I went in, and I like being clean!"

He was "a man of one book." Smith was clothed with the Spirit of God because he was a man given to the Word of God and prayer.

Some well-meaning inquirers asked Smith Wigglesworth about his prayer life. They said, "Smith Wigglesworth, you're a man of faith and miracles; you've raised people from the dead. You've cast out demons. How long do you pray each day?"

"Well," Smith replied, "I don't ever pray any longer than twenty minutes."

"What?" They were confused at his answer; they assumed he prayed much longer.

After a short pause, Smith Wigglesworth continued, "Yes, but I never go twenty minutes without praying."[3]

KATHRYN KUHLMAN—SECRET ENTRANCE TO THE AIRPORT

It is reported that near Kathryn Kuhlman's home in Pittsburgh, the airport provided a separate entrance for her in the gateway. Why? The power of God was so resident on her when she walked through the airport terminal many would fall out in the Spirit. In order to avoid the pandemonium, the authorities let her enter the airport through a side door. They did this to keep her away from the throngs of people.

On another occasion while at a hotel, she walked through the kitchen area and all of the cooks and servers in the kitchen fell out under the power of God. What caused these responses to her presence? She was given to a life of prayer—she prayed constantly.[4]

Sadly, the Church knows very little of such power. We will spend a few minutes with God in prayer and expect signs and wonders to take place. This is not the formula for success. In fact, it leads to frustration, defeat, stagnation, impotency, and eventually burnout.

Prayer breathes life into the whole realm of your world. In fact, everything we know and love will be impacted by a praying individual and church—nothing is left untouched. The whole realm of your life will become better, yielding desirable fruit for the Father and giving you and your church the much-needed strength and wisdom to accomplish the will of God.

> *The whole realm of your life will become better, yielding desirable fruit for the Father.*

UNLESS WE AWAKEN

|| 7 ||

THE MOUNTAIN IS SLEEPING

*We have taught a generation to feast and play
but the times demand we fast and pray.*
—LOU ENGLE

One day Napoleon was having a strategic meeting with his top generals and trusted advisors. While looking at a map, he was reflecting on the nations and territories his great army had conquered. He approached a map that was on the table; there he paused for a moment, then he ran his index finger round a great country and said, "There lies a sleeping giant. *Let it sleep!*" He was referring to the massive country of China.

Likewise, I can see satan following Napoleon's example. While looking at the globe, he points his finger at the Church and warns his workers, "Leave her alone, *let her sleep!* Don't wake her. If she ever discovers the power of prayer, our dominance will be over. Let her sleep."

HOT LAVA

I think volcanoes are spectacular yet very mysterious. The brute power of an erupting volcano has very few equals on the earth. Today, volcanoes are sprinkled all over the planet, on dry ground as well as within the depths of the ocean. They are geographical wonders that leave one awestruck at their size and disastrous potential. Recently, the headline from a *Forbes* magazine article in March of 2021 read, "Mauna Loa, the World's Biggest Volcano, Is Waking Up and It's Time to Prep for an Eruption." So many things catch my eye in that headline—words like *waking up, prep, eruption.* I believe the Lord is releasing a prophetic utterance across our land that is speaking the same thing about His Church. Do you sense it as well? And interestingly enough, the last six words of the article are, "Mauna Loa is slowly waking up."[1] I believe the Church is as well!

FOUR TYPES OF VOLCANOES

Currently, volcanoes all over the earth are waking up. According to the United States Geological Survey there are 161 potentially active volcanoes in the United States and its territories and over 1,300 worldwide.[2] By anyone's standard that is a significant number of rumbling mountains that could blow their top. History records the world's most devastating volcano explosion took place in 1815 in Tambora, Indonesia. It is estimated that it took the lives of nearly 100,000 people, with the majority of those deaths coming as a result of starvation due to the aftermath of the eruption.[3]

Scientists have identified four classes of volcanoes: extinct, dormant, active, and erupting.

Extinct

If scientists do not expect a volcano to ever erupt again, they consider it to be extinct. An extinct volcano by definition is a dead volcano that no longer has a lava supply. It has not erupted in hundreds, if not thousands, of years and is not expected to. An extinct volcano is not a threat to its surroundings, neighboring cities, or the environment. It may look like a volcano, but it has no fire.

Dormant

In a dormant volcano there is lava deep within its bowels, but is considered inactive. Dormant volcanoes have not erupted for a very long time but may erupt at a future time. This type of volcano is waiting until conditions are right to erupt, which is why they are often called sleeping giants. Before 1980, scientists considered Mount St. Helens in Washington a dormant volcano, but it erupted with a fury on May 18, 1980, and left fifty-seven people dead and billions of dollars in damage in its wake. The entire nation and the world felt its explosive impact.

Active

Volcanologists have loosely defined an active volcano as having a recent history of erupting and the likelihood of another eruption is probable. This means the volcano is alive, it has life, and at some level is operating like a volcano.

Erupting

Erupting volcanoes come in various sizes and impact. In fact, some eruptions are uneventful and can be quite calm. On the other hand, some eruptions can contribute to earthquakes and at the same time discharge molten lava high into the sky, causing fascinating light storms around and above the mountain. In addition, dangerous lava flows from the lip of the volcano are hazardous to the environment as well as people.

Obviously, the active and erupting volcanoes are the two most dangerous; they are best positioned to have an explosive impact. However, you cannot rule out the other two—they are still called volcanoes for a reason and have the potential to come alive again.

What does this have to do with prayer?

Everything!

It has been said that a volcano is just a mountain until it is not. There comes a time when the mountain decides to release its smoke, fire, and lava, and at that moment everything changes, not only for the mountain but its surroundings. And I might add, there is nothing on earth that can stop its energy and power; everything gives way to its fury.

In a lot of ways I find these categories—*extinct, dormant, active,* and *erupting*—perfect descriptions of the types of churches around the world. Every church should be able to identify which description best fits them. For example, some churches have no lava flow whatsoever and the possibility is nonexistent. Meanwhile, some churches are like dormant volcanoes—the fire is lying beneath the surface with the possibility of being released. Others, like the active volcano, have erupted at one time but have lost their strength. However, they can spew lava and impact the world again. The most significant one is the erupting volcano. It is actively breathing fire, and people come from everywhere to see and experience its splendor.

Fortunately, we serve a God who loves His Church and He desires for it to be revived. Our prayer meetings must address the dormancy and inactivity of local congregations. God will respond and release her glorious power upon the earth.

> **We serve a God who loves His Church and He desires for it to be revived.**

Every day, pray these five things over your church:

- God, please forgive us from drifting from You. We give You permission to wake us up, all of us.

Therefore He says: "Awake, you who sleep, arise from the dead, and Christ will give you light" (Ephesians 5:14 NKJV).

- We pray that the leadership and all church members would grow increasingly dissatisfied with their current walk with You and would cry out for more of You.

O God, You are my God; early will I seek You; my soul thirsts for You; my flesh longs for You in a dry and thirsty land where there is no water (Psalm 63:1 NKJV).

- Reveal to each of us anything in our lives that offends, grieves, or quenches Your Spirit. We will be quick to repent.

I seek you with all my heart; do not let me stray from your commands (Psalm 119:10 NIV).

Search me, God, and know my heart; test me and know my anxious thoughts. See if there is any offensive way in me, and lead me in the way everlasting (Psalm 139:23-24 NIV).

- As we seek Your face, may Your presence and glory increase in our church services.

Lord, I have loved the habitation of Your house, and the place where Your glory dwells (Psalm 26:8 NKJV).

- Baptize all of us with the Holy Spirit and fire.

I indeed baptize you with water unto repentance, but He who is coming after me is mightier than I... He will baptize you with the Holy Spirit and fire (Matthew 3:11 NKJV).

|| 8 ||

THE ENEMY IS US

*Don't pray when it rains if you don't
pray when the sun shines.*
—SATCHEL PAIGE

Walt Kelly, an American animator and cartoonist, gave the
world the funny animal comic strip "Pogo." The pop-
ular printed cartoon became Kelly's platform for political
and philosophical commentary. One feature he drew gar-
nered him worldwide accolades. He was drawing a comic to
commemorate Earth Day in 1971. Kelly drew Pogo and his
friend sitting on the extension of a tree root and with sad-
dened, confused, and somewhat angry faces. The two of them
were looking at an immense amount of discarded trash on
the forest floor. Pogo said, "Yep, son, we have met the enemy
and he is us."

Pogo realized there was no one else to blame for the dis-
gusting volume of trash on the once beautiful forest floor.

This reality startled him, but this moment was necessary so humanity could fix the problem. Humans threw out the trash and must accept the responsibility.

As Ecclesiastes tells us, there is *"A time to weep, and a time to laugh; a time to mourn, and a time to dance"* (Ecclesiastes 3:4 NIV).

Even though there is some discrepancy of thought regarding what constitutes a generation, many biblical scholars assume a generation is approximately 40 years in length.[1] If we use 40 years as our reference, there have been around fifty generations to live and die since the time of Christ.

With that being said, no other generation in the history of the world has had greater potential, opportunity, intellect, and resources to touch and reach the world than this generation. No generation has heard more sermons, attended more conferences, acquired more degrees, and participated in more worship services than this generation. No generation has gone through more deliverance sessions and prayer lines, and we have definitely had more hands laid on top of our heads than any other people.

> *No other generation in the history of the world has had greater potential, opportunity, intellect, and resources to touch and reach the world than this generation.*

According to statistical data, it is estimated at the time of Christ 300,000,000 people inhabited the earth.[2] Currently, the population of the United States is now pushing 400,000,000. Across the globe, nearly three billion people identify as Christian. In light of the above data, Christianity should be spreading rapidly and overtaking the world. But this is not the case—far from it.

One has to ask the question: "How is that possible?" The spiritual resources in our hands are unlike anything the world has ever experienced. For example, we have the fire of the Holy Spirit that has been passed down from generation to generation. We have the full release of the fivefold ministry—apostle, pastor, teacher, prophet, and evangelist. We have all the gifts of the Holy Spirit at our fingertips. We have 27 books of the New Testament that outline clean, pure doctrine; righteous living; and demonstrations of spirit—not to mention all the other books that have been written about the Bible, the Holy Spirit, and His gifts. There is no excuse; we lack nothing. Then why are we not experiencing all that God has for us? Maybe this generation of believers fully embody what Paul warned his beloved Timothy—there will be a church that has *"a form of godliness but denying its power"* (2 Timothy 3:5 NIV).

We have to do better; we have no excuse. Look at what we have been given—authority to use His name, the two-edged sword in our mouths, the full armor of God, plus the mandate and power to lay hands on the sick and even cast out devils. God has given us everything to accomplish His will for the earth. When the Church operates in this realm of authority and power, the enemy may oppose it, but he cannot stop it! Listen, where we are as a society—it's not God's fault. Perhaps we need to take a hard look at ourselves and what we have done with what He has given us and admit, like Pogo, "Yep, son, we have met the enemy and he is us."

> When the Church operates in this realm of authority and power, the enemy may oppose it, but he cannot stop it!

The late John Osteen who understood our weighty responsibility often said, "Hell is too hot, heaven is too real, eternity is too long, and my responsibility is too great for me to fail Him in this hour." When operating from a place of prayer and under the power of the fullness of the Holy Spirit, history proves the forces of darkness cannot keep the gospel from advancing. So our worst enemy is us. We are the ones who determine the degree of the Kingdom of God's reach and effectiveness.

People have said that in this dispensation of grace what I am suggesting is unnecessary, extreme, over-the-top, too much, and an offense to the "rest" we have in Jesus. I beg to differ, and for that matter the apostle Paul would stoutly resist such logic. If you disagree, please do us all a great service and search the Holy Scriptures and find us another plan or pathway that gets Kingdom-conquering results like the early Church experienced.

Let me help you—there isn't another way. The Church triumphantly advances while it is on its knees. The only plan that works is the plan that worked in the book of Acts. Lest we forget, it was a small band of praying people who "turned the world upside down" in a few short years.

Leonard Ravenhill recalled something Dr. J.B. Phillips, author of the Phillips New Testament, once said about the beginning of Acts:

> The book of Acts describes the Church of Jesus Christ before it became fat and out of breath by prosperity, and muscle-bound by over-organization. This was the Church where people were not forced to sign articles of faith, instead, they acted in faith. Here was the place where worshippers did not "say" prayers, they prayed in the Holy Ghost. ...These folk did not gather together a group of intellectuals to study psycho-somatic medicine, they simply healed the sick![3]

WHAT HAPPENS WHEN WE DON'T PRAY?

Praying men have been God's deputies on earth…
prayerless men have never been used of him.
—E.M. BOUNDS

Think with me for a moment—I need you to let the following thoughts sink into your soul. According to the Bible, God is all-powerful and has the capacity to do whatever He wants, whenever He wants to do it. He has no limitations or rival. His might is unmatchable and His knowledge is endless. He is everywhere at all times. He has created all things and holds all things together by His word. Yet it is this God who subjects Himself to the prayers of His children. Seems odd, doesn't it?

One of the greatest missionaries of all time was Hudson Taylor. He had a tremendous impact on the world but especially China in the late 1800s. He founded the China Inland

Mission, and during his ministry he launched 125 schools. In a book titled *Hudson Taylor's Spiritual Secret* written by his son and daughter-in-law, Howard Taylor wrote of his father, "For forty years the sun never rose on China a single day that God didn't find him on his knees."[1] Hudson Taylor's prayers moved God for China.

Have you ever wondered why our 21st-century version of Christianity looks different from the first-century version?

Today, it would seem we have much more physical talent than the early disciples, better trained orators, definitely more educated preachers, obviously we have better facilities, greater technology, we understand cultural shifts and generational trends, and without question we are more organized. However, their expression of Christianity is not the same as our expression. Why is there a difference?

Here is the secret, and it really isn't a secret at all—they prayed! They didn't just talk about prayer—they prayed. They prioritized it, longed for it, focused on it, promoted it, and gathered for it. However, for the most part the 21st-century Church dabbles in it.

If we are honest, most of us find it difficult to pray. C.S. Lewis in *Letters to Malcolm: Chiefly on Prayer* describes what many feel about prayer.

> Well, let's now at any rate come clean. Prayer is irksome. An excuse to omit it is never unwelcome. When it is over, this casts a feeling of relief and holiday over the rest of the day. We

are reluctant to begin. We are delighted to finish. While we are at prayer, but not while we are reading a novel or solving a crossword puzzle, any trifle is enough to distract us. And we know that we are not alone in this.[2]

Becoming faithful at prayer is not easy. Our flesh fights prayer because it loathes anything that requires isolation and discipline. Plus, the enemy of our soul, the devil, discourages us from praying because he knows the heavenly power that it releases. The combination of these two assaults can at times seem to be insurmountable.

> *Our flesh fights prayer because it loathes anything that requires isolation and discipline.*

SHE HAD POWER AVAILABLE

There was a lady who lived way out in the country for years without any electricity, but finally the power company was able to get electricity installed where she lived. But after several months, the power company noticed that very little power was being used at this woman's home. They did some tests and saw that the power was getting to her house just fine, but she didn't seem to be using much at all. So a representative decided to visit her home and ask if there was a problem.

"Ma'am, are you using your electricity here that we've run to your property?" he asked.

"Oh, yes!" she replied. "It's been very helpful."

"Can you explain to me how you use your new electric power?"

"Well, it's very simple," she said. "When it begins to get dark, I turn on the lights long enough to light my kerosene lamps, and then I turn the lights off again."

This precious lady evidently did not understand the potential and power available to her and her home. She had access to all the power she could ever use, but failed to fully utilize it. The irony of the story is remarkable when compared to the power of prayer.

Two of the most powerful forces on the planet are prayerfulness and prayerlessness. Both of these are dynamic in their working. Leonard Ravenhill said, "The true man of God is heartsick, grieved at the worldliness of the Church… grieved at the toleration of sin in the Church, grieved at the prayerlessness in the Church."[3]

Let's focus on prayerlessness for a moment.

What is prayerlessness? It is the state of not praying, in other words, failing to pray. This doesn't mean a person doesn't pray at all, but the overall prayer life is minimal at best. They are not committed to the task of praying. Pastor Ronnie Floyd in his book *How to Pray* said there are two major statements about prayer that we must understand: "Prayer occurs when you depend on God" and "Prayerlessness occurs when you depend on yourself."[4]

Prayerlessness is both dangerous and irresponsible; dreadful results occur when we neglect prayer. Where there is little prayer there is little power. When prayer is absent there is a lack of supernatural power and the enemy advances freely. According to the Bible, prayerlessness is not mere weakness—it is sin.

Moreover, as for me, far be it from me that I should sin against the Lord in ceasing to pray for you (1 Samuel 12:23 NKJV).

> **Where there is little prayer there is little power.**

It Restricts God's Hand

Some would say that failing to pray is an indicator of a lack of focus and concern for the advancement of Christ's Kingdom on earth. I know that is a strong statement and may be offensive; however, think about the ramifications when we don't pray. For example, when a person or church minimizes prayer, it suspends the will of God from being done on the earth. Let that truth sink in—His will is suspended, held back due to a lack of prayer. This is frightening because it has both temporal and eternal consequences. What things are delayed? Good things, helpful things, life-giving things, and supernatural things are postponed due to our lack of prayer. We restrict the hand of God when we don't pray; however, when we do pray the Kingdom advances, hope comes, lives are changed, the gospel advances. But once again, when we don't, the opposite takes place. In all honesty, the fruit of our prayerlessness is real; we see the results every day. The growing evil in the world today can be traced back to the lack of emphasis placed on prayer.

We have to be honest. Prayerlessness is prevalent at all levels within the body of Christ.

There are two major reasons believers do not pray effectively and consistently. First, prayer has been seen as an "alternative" plan rather than a necessity—why? Perhaps our religious overtones of phrases like "He is in control" or "He is sovereign" have had a subliminal effect on us. We have heard these phrases so much we take a mental posture that God has my best interests at heart, therefore He will "handle it all for me." We basically utter to ourselves, "He is in control, so I will flow with whatever happens." The net result has opened the door for the enemy to take advantage of our passivity and advance his purposes in our lives and the ones we love.

Second, people are extremely busy and find it difficult to add another thing to their taxing schedules. This is true, but prayer is still necessary and must become a priority for each of us. Charles Haddon Spurgeon described the weekly prayer meeting as "the heating apparatus of the church."

Show me a church that doesn't pray and I will show you a church with no genuine spiritual fire. They may have flash—spiritual sparklers if you will. They may even have excitement, enthusiasm, programs, and a lot of activity, but I promise you they will not have Holy Spirit fire. The prayer level of the church determines the fire level in the church. That's why some churches are cold and frigid—no prayer! No fire!

> **The prayer level of the church determines the fire level in the church.**

Most, if not all, that God does on the earth He does in direct response to prayer. The comings and the goings of the Kingdom of God on the earth are a direct reaction to and reflection of the prayers of His children. Prayerlessness, or weak praying and even unbelieving prayer, restrains God's power and disables His desirous interaction with mankind and their conditions. The greatest gift to a community, town, or village is a praying church. It alone can change the trajectory and history of a people.

Dr. Lewis Drummond said, "Our lack of prayer has exacted a tremendous toll. Spiritual immaturity, ministry ineptness, poverty of power—not to mention the strife, division, sin, and animosity in the churches—is the price we pay for our neglect of disciplined private and corporate prayer."[5]

The churches who are not praying have lost significant ground and influence in the cities they were called to reach. They too have lost influence with God. Talent is not what God is looking for when it comes to His power being released upon an individual. No, God's eye and ear is looking and listening for one thing—the individual who prays.

Now My eyes will be open and My ears atten-tive to prayer made in this place (2 Chronicles 7:15 NKJV).

Could it be that our churches are suffering because there is no viable prayer ministry both personally and within the church? When prayer is underemphasized, the natural will supersede the supernatural, and evil will triumph over good every time. The Holy Spirit's work and activity is directly and proportionately tied to prayer.

Andrew Murray had a word for the pastors of his day and I think it applies to us as well: "The indispensable thing is not preaching, not pastoral visitation, not church work, but fellowship with God in prayer till they are clothed with power from on high."[6] Can you imagine what would happen in our churches if prayer was the highest priority of every minister?

Jesus taught that, *"Men ought always to pray"* (Luke 18:1 NKJV). God is not limited by human hands or conditions. He is well able to overcome all that man has, but there is one thing that limits His activity on the earth—it is prayer-lessness. God instructs His children to pray, and hundreds of the recorded stories in the Bible are His reactions to their prayers and cries for intervention.

We receive when we pray. Without prayer we flow like a leaf downstream and the current takes us where it wills; how-ever, prayer brings God's interaction and power into our cir-cumstances. It changes everything. Prayer is literally working in conjunction with God to accomplish His purposes on the earth.

Call to Me, and I will answer you, and show you great and mighty things, which you do not know (Jeremiah 33:3 NKJV).

> **Prayer brings God's interaction and power into our circumstances. It changes everything.**

Thomas Watson, a Puritan preacher in the 17th century, said, "Christ was in an agony at prayer (Luke 22:44). Many when they pray are rather in a lethargy, than in an agony. When they are about the world, they are all fire; when they are at prayer, they are all ice."[7] Dreadful results occur when we neglect prayer, and the least not being that the enemy advances freely in all points of society.

They Prayed for Ten Days

Let us not forget Jesus launched the first-ever New Testament Church with a prayer meeting. Yep, that's right. Sounds so basic and unappealing, doesn't it? No fanfare, no flashy marketing blitz, nothing more than a small group who secluded themselves in a confined space—the upper room. They prayed and worshiped God for ten days and then heaven came and the earth has never been the same.

Those ten days of intentional prayer released the power and fire of God into the Church. We know God never does things haphazardly or on a whim; He has purpose in all that He does. He sent a message to the Church and all church ministries to follow—prayer is the foundation of all moves of God. God delivered the blueprint to the Church. This was His way, the perfect way of launching, building, and expanding the Kingdom of God—*prayer!* This humble yet penetrating pattern was locked into place—God's method.

God has tied Himself to prayer. Prayer is the way He chose to intervene in the affairs of men—He is tethered to it. He is released by it or limited due to the lack of it. In fact, prayerlessness has great power—it can prevent a soul from being saved, a body healed, a prodigal from coming home, or even keep a church from being revived. Prayerlessness can actually delay and even defeat the purposes of God.

> **Prayerlessness can actually delay and even defeat the purposes of God.**

If prayer is His method of releasing Kingdom power then why is it that the Church struggles so mightily with it? Why do most churches underemphasize this essential element of the heart of God? Tragically, prayerlessness is the greatest misstep of the modern Church. History has revealed to us that if we fail here then we will fail everywhere else; dreadful things are its byproduct. All of the work of the Kingdom hinges on prayer; there is absolutely no substitute for it.

|| 10 ||

THE EARTH SHOOK

I fear the prayers of John Knox more than
all the assembled armies of Europe.
— MARY, QUEEN OF SCOTS

D id you know on a yearly basis the US Geological Survey
identifies nearly 500,000 earthquakes worldwide?[1] That is
close to 1,400 earthquakes a day. Obviously, most quakes are
not large enough to even be felt by us, but they do register at
some level on the seismograph.

The most deadly earthquake in history was in Shaanxi,
China in 1556. Its destructive power was so severe it is estimated to have killed 830,000 people.[2] Throughout history
researchers believe over thirteen million people have lost
their lives due to earthquakes.

When was the last time you heard about an earthquake
and nothing catastrophic occurred, only positive things?
There were at least three earthquakes like this that took

place in the New Testament. Each had positive effects. They were not environmentally or physically destructive. Let's take a quick look at the three earthquakes.

The first earthquake in the New Testament occurred when Jesus died on the cross.

Then, behold, the veil of the temple was torn in two from top to bottom; and the earth quaked, and the rocks were split, and the graves were opened; and many bodies of the saints who had fallen asleep were raised; and coming out of the graves after His resurrection, they went into the holy city and appeared to many (Matthew 27:51-53 NKJV).

In this text there is no record of anyone being hurt or dying; it was totally an expression of the moment when the death of Jesus rattled the ground. The text reveals that as a result of the quaking many came up out of their graves and walked around the city. Can you imagine what impact that had on Jerusalem?

In fact, as a result of the earthquake and all that he witnessed, a centurion soldier who was guarding the body of Jesus declared, *"Truly this was the Son of God!"* (Matthew 27:54 NKJV).

In full transparency, the earthquake did do some necessary and measured damage to the temple—it rent the temple curtain, symbolizing that Jesus was clearing the way for man to have unfettered access to God.

The second earthquake accompanied the resurrection of Jesus.

Now after the Sabbath, as the first day of the week began to dawn, Mary Magdalene and the other Mary came to see the tomb. And behold, there was a great earthquake; for an angel of the Lord descended from heaven, and came and rolled back the stone from the door, and sat on it (Matthew 28:1-2 NKJV).

It is here that Jesus walked victoriously from the depths of hell with the keys of death, hell, and the grave in His hands. He burst through death's domain and stood triumphant over its grip. The earth shook!

The third earthquake's epicenter was a prison. According to the narrative, nothing outside the prison was affected. Let me explain what happened.

Paul and Silas were en route to a prayer meeting when a young girl who was following them repeatedly proclaimed these men were servants of the most High God. Having discerned she was under the influence of a divination spirit, Paul commanded for it to come out of her, and it did. This upset the city's most influential businesspeople who used this girl's ability to gain much profit. Those who benefited from her sorcery persuaded the political and religious leaders to have Paul and Silas beaten with rods. Afterward, they were placed into the inner part of the prison with their legs fastened with chains.

Recovering from the severe beating, at midnight Paul and Silas began to pray and sing hymns unto the Lord. Acts 16:26 (NKJV) says, *"Suddenly there was a great earthquake, so that the foundations of the prison were shaken."* Do you wonder what caused the earth to rumble? I don't believe it was coincidental. I am fully persuaded their prayers and praise so touched God that His reaction caused the prison to shake violently. The quaking was so intense that it shook the very foundations of the prison, which caused the locked doors to swing open and chains and shackles to fall off Paul and Silas.

This was no ordinary earthquake. It was powerful, but again, from what we understand the quaking and the effects were limited to the prison only. There is no record of panic or activity outside the prison. In fact, the narrative implies that no one on the outside ever knew what happened inside the prison until the next morning.

What caused the earth to quake? The answer is found in Acts 16:25 (NKJV):

> *But at midnight Paul and Silas were praying and singing hymns to God, and the prisoners were listening to them.*

They prayed! Look at what happened when Paul and Silas prayed:

1. The earth quaked.

2. The foundations shook.

3. The doors opened.

4. Chains and shackles unlocked.

5. Those who were asleep woke up.

These five things happened because of a prayer meeting. And I feel strongly that these same things can happen to us, our churches, and our communities when we begin to take prayer seriously.

I love the fact there was an earthquake, but I love even more that the earthquake was strong enough to shake and rattle the foundation of the prison. Foundations represent structure, stability, things that are fixed, embedded, and immovable.

There are different levels of earthquakes. Some you don't even feel; at other times you can feel the earth rumble, the lamps and trinkets on the table shift, and the picture frames on the wall tilt. Then there are those earthquakes that dislodge, displace, and bring destruction to stable structures. This is the type of a move of God we need—not just a move that affects the surface but one that dislodges and disrupts unhealthy foundations.

> *This is the type of a move of God we need—not just a move that affects the surface but one that dislodges and disrupts unhealthy foundations.*

Prophetically, the current prayer movement of our churches at best may cause a slight rumbling but nothing that the devil has to worry about. Why? Typically, the prayer ministry of the church gets minimal attention and in most cases is the least attended; therefore, the spiritual quaking coming from our prayer meetings is not strong enough to affect the foundations of our culture, community, schools, government, and even the lives of those we are called to minister to. This has to change!

Prayer alone can only do this. R.A. Torrey once said, "Every real revival in the Church has been the child of prayer. There have been revivals without much preaching; there have been revivals with absolutely no organization; but there has never been a mighty revival without mighty praying."[3] And Dwight L. Moody adds, "Every great movement of God can be traced to a kneeling figure."[4]

Diligent prayer affects both God and the devil. Prayer opens doors and shuts them as well. Prayer makes things happen and also stops things that are already in motion. Prayer is not the only weapon we have in our arsenal, but it is the catalyst for all the other armor God has given us. It is the key ingredient to the work of God on the earth. It must precede every ministry endeavor the Church pursues.

Recently as I spoke to our church family I said, "We don't need more preaching, more conferences, more worship nights; we need more prayer meetings." I strongly concur all the above are good things, but we have tried them and yet our culture hasn't been greatly impacted by our efforts. I am not the only one who believes this, William Reid said it this way, "Why is there so much speaking, yet so little prayer? Why is there so much running to and fro, yet so little prayer? Why so much bustle and business, yet so little prayer? Why so many meetings with our fellow-men, yet so few meetings with God?"[5]

Thankfully, we are painfully discovering our effectiveness is not found in the public meetings, but in the private prayer closet. Jesus told us the secret of ministry power in Matthew 6:6 (NKJV), *"But you, when you pray, go into your room, and when you have shut your door, pray to your Father who is in the secret place; and your Father who sees in secret will reward you openly."*

Without delay, we need to shift our energy and emphasis to the prayer meeting, and then when we are faithful there, God will demonstrate unprecedented power in the public arena. This is what He said He would do: "Meet with Me in private and I will reward you openly" (see Matthew 6:6).

Evan Roberts said, "Prayer is the secret of power."

|| 11 ||

PRAYER IS A BLOODY BATTLEGROUND

Prayer is the best weapon we possess. It is
the key that opens the heart of God.
—St. Padre Pio

War is bloody. There are casualties in every conflict. War requires great sacrifice from each soldier. Today, there are two kingdoms at war; they are not physical kingdoms that you see with your eyes, but spiritual kingdoms. These two kingdoms are led by opposing leaders—satan the prince of darkness and Jesus the Prince of Light. Both leaders have a significant invisible army that manifests absolute loyalty to their master. With resolve each army seeks to advance their leader's agenda for the world. It is no secret both satan and Jesus desire all humans to worship them.

We who belong to Jesus are His children and our aim is to advance the Kingdom of God upon the earth. However, satan and his children and demons oppose that agenda and seek to advance their power as well. It is good for us to realize that even though we live in the flesh and have our earthly struggles, we are ultimately at war with satan and his invisible forces.

> *For we do not wrestle against flesh and blood, but against principalities, against powers, against the rulers of the darkness of this age, against spiritual hosts of wickedness in the heavenly places. Therefore take up the whole armor of God, that you may be able to withstand in the evil day, and having done all, to stand* (Ephesians 6:12-13 NKJV).

The demonic activity in the world is real, it is highly organized, and with relative ease it is fortifying its dominance in our society. They have taken satan's mantra of "steal, kill, and destroy" literally. They have not wavered at their assignment. Every day we witness the world suffocating from the darkness emanating from his kingdom. Christians have to realize the forces of evil will show no mercy as they relentlessly seek bondage, carnage, and destruction for all humans. It is no secret one of satan's ultimate goals is to dominate the entire human race.

Warning: When believers do not take their battle position of prayer, we actually neutralize the work of God—it slows down or comes to a stop. God moves when His children pray, but when we don't pray the opposite is true. The net result has unimaginable consequences. Furthermore, inattention to prayer actually gives place to the devil to advance his cause and evil. Without resistance, precious territory is lost. In addition, the gains the Church has achieved over the years are surrendered to satan's ever-advancing spiritual and natural armies. Due to prayerlessness, the influence of the Church has been pushed into the corner.

> **Due to prayerlessness, the influence of the Church has been pushed into the corner.**

However, when Christians pray effectively heavenly angels are dispatched to aid the human servants who are advancing the cause of Christ (see Daniel 10; Hebrews 1:14). Territory is gained or retaken as souls are saved, and unreached people groups hear the message of Jesus for the first time. The spiritual and moral climate shifts back to a level of civility and decency. Law and order are reestablished. Churches become awakened and the Spirit of God sparks revival in communities. The light of Jesus dispels darkness and the Kingdom of God gloriously advances.

Without belaboring the point, we have to take prayer seriously. We can no longer treat it lightly. Prayer is the doorway for God's intervention with man. The devil knows this and works feverishly to keep us away from it. E.M.

Bounds said, "A person who can pray is the mightiest instrument Christ has in the world." A person who can pray is the mightiest instrument Christ has in this world. A praying Church is stronger than all the gates of hell.

As history proves, with any war there are struggles, surprises, and missteps. There are advances and retreats, giving and taking, wins and loses. In the midst of this epic struggle, we are instructed to not lose heart when things are difficult and we seem to be making little to no progress (see 2 Thessalonians 3:13).

If we know the only answer to satan's reach is prayer then why don't we pray? Recently I heard a small portion of a message the late David Wilkerson preached on prayer. I think it provides a good response to my question. My heart was convicted as my spirit clung to every word he spoke. Below is a partial transcript of his message.

> Only praying men touch God. Very few of God's people pray any more. We are too busy working for Jesus to talk to Him. You see Christ coming to the office—standing outside the office door and He says, "Man of God, can I have an hour please?"
>
> "Not now, Lord, I have a counseling session, I have got to go try to save a marriage."
>
> Again the Spirit of God calls, "Man of God, may I have an hour with you?"

"Not now, Lord, I am meeting with my architect and the building committee for Your new church. We'll be busy until midnight."

Again the Lord calls, "What about tomorrow? May I have even one day with you now?"

"Not now, Lord, I have no time. I am leaving for South Africa for a missions conference. Very soon, Lord, but not just now—souls are dying and I am needed in Africa."

We have time to visit, to build, to travel, to vacation, to attend meetings, for recreation, reading, counseling, visitation, but no time to pray. You know I am weary hearing people say, "This is such a busy, fast-paced generation we don't have time to pray today." It is not a lack of time it is a lack of desire. You will make time for what you really want to do. Look at those Christian brothers on the racquetball court sweating, concentrating, spending hours and hours on the racquetball court. Next thing you know he's got a Coke in hand and he's got sandwiches, probably gonna watch three hours of cowboy time. These are the men who tell me they have no time to pray. And here's a dear lady, she spends her time with Tupperware. She has business hours. Tomorrow she's going shopping and in the afternoon she's gotta see what happens to Laura on TV. She tells me she has no time to pray. Look at the young people in America wasting their time playing Pacman, galaxy war, goofing off, bored, restless, looking for action, but no time to pray. Oh, God, somehow get this generation on its knees. Break it. Not just the Lord's prayer but a Holy Ghost communion.

You say you have no time to pray, yet today the Son of God who has to care for all the multiplied universes—He has the time to pray for you. He takes the time to intercede before the throne of God—He prays. You say you have no time—He does. We'll go anywhere, we'll do anything in His name but we will not pray. We'll sing in a choir, but we won't pray. We'll visit the sick and the prisoner, but we won't pray. We'll counsel the hurting and we'll stay up all night to counsel a friend, we won't pray. We will fight corruption, but we won't pray. We will crusade for morality, but we won't pray. We will stand up against nuclear armaments, but we won't pray. We can sit here for two hours praising God, but we won't go home and pray. We will attend crusades and seminars, go from meeting to meeting, lift our hands and sing and shout and praise the Lord, but we don't pray.

Prayer is not just a bunch of words running out of our mouths. It's not just a bunch of people just saying words. No wonder the devil is sampling the spiritual strength of this generation because prayer is a bloody battleground. Prayer is a bloody battleground! I believe the devil will throw hell at any man who says, "I'm going to pray and seek the face of God." The devil is not afraid of power hungry saints, but he trembles at the sound of a praying saint.[1]

TALK IS CHEAP

When discussing the value of prayer, everyone nods their head in agreement that prayer is important. But it is something entirely different to actually engage in spiritual warfare by praying. We have to move beyond words. Believers everywhere have to be sober minded about prayer—prayer is *battle* it isn't for the faint of heart!

Prayer is a call to battle. When a pastor summons their church to pray, they are calling the church to war. Jonathan Falwell recently wrote, "Churches must move beyond the cursory nod to prayer and return to the days of powerful, yet arduous, prayer meetings. Prayer, the way God intends, is hard work."[2] As Oswald Chambers said, "Prayer is not a preparation for the battle; it is the battle!" He added, "What has hell to fear other than a God-anointed, prayer-powered Church?"

Personal prayer as well as church-wide prayer meetings no longer can be on the fringes of our schedules. The prayer meeting can't be marginalized or something we attend if we have "nothing else to do." If we are to see a substantial and sustained move of God in our churches and communities, prayer must be at the center of our existence. This will require significant sacrifices and adjustments.

There is a subtle yet powerful and seductive undercurrent flowing through the Church of Jesus that communicates that intensive corporate prayer is unnecessary. Some in this camp call it extreme, too much, laborious, work-oriented, and over the top. If we do not answer the call to prayer then our society will continue its steady slide into darkness and the Church's impact will be nothing more than a memory. The army of satan is advancing at the speed of light and the Church must awaken in order to neutralize satan's growing influence. This is not done through a political agenda or church-growth strategy; it is done through prayer and prayer alone.

UNLESS WE TRAVAIL

12

IT CAN BE A MATTER OF LIFE OR DEATH

*Not to pray because you do not feel fit
to pray is like saying, "I will not take
medicine because I am too ill."*
—CHARLES SPURGEON

I believe most Christians eagerly want to learn to pray effectively; however, to be honest, most of us struggle at it. We start and stop; therefore, we don't maintain consistency. And one of the reasons for this is that we don't understand the full purpose of prayer. In order to progress, we have to grasp the value of prayer and why God wants us to pray. And if we truly understood the earthly and eternal purpose of prayer, more of us would truly pray.

With that being said, one of the most difficult jobs a pastor has is to rally their people to pray corporately. The enemy fights this emphasis at every level. The devil knows he can't stop the preaching of the Word in our churches, and he knows he can't keep people from gathering to worship the Lord. Those two practices are entrenched into the DNA of church life. However, the one thing that is the supernatural catalyst to both preaching and worship is prayer, and the devil hates it.

Pastor Kim Owens of Fresh Start Church shares in her book *Doorkeepers of Revival* how corporate prayer changed a nation. Jackson Senyong from Uganda explained what happened when an evil regime took over his nation.

> In our desperation the devil made us pray. See, revival comes to us either from desperation or devastation. We choose the way we want revival. People in Uganda began to pray like dying people. These are the kinds of prayers that bring revival, not casual prayers. Prayer was not an event for us, it was a lifestyle. We put demands on heaven to open and on the heart of God to respond. Prayer must be taken to that melting point. ...Prayer must be able to outcry the sin of the land before revival comes! When the sin of the city is crying louder than the voice of intercession, we will never see a new day of transformation. In America, you are accustomed to events; therefore, you do not know how fervent prayer can be sustained. Event praying is hit

and run praying and when we run the enemy is occupying. Those prayers do not bring revival.[1]

Without apology, I believe of all the ministries and responsibilities assigned to the people of God, none is more important than corporate prayer. To me this is the highest calling of the Church; however, as sad as it is, nothing is more ignored by the church than prayer. We have done everything well—we planned, we organized, we strategized, we trained, we rehearsed, we won souls, but we stopped praying.

> *Of all the ministries and responsibilities assigned to the people of God none is more important than corporate prayer.*

Charles H. Spurgeon, who has been called the prince of preachers, once said in a sermon, "The condition of the church may be very accurately gauged by its prayer meetings." He added, "The prayer-meeting must be maintained at all cost."[2] Never has a statement been truer. According to Spurgeon, the prayer meeting was the spiritual thermometer of the church. He regarded his Monday night prayer meeting as the most important meeting of the week.

A DISTURBANCE IS NEEDED

Catherine Booth once said, "If we want a better future we must disturb the present." The very fact that you are reading this book indicates you are not fully happy with the present and are ready to disturb it. We have no other choice—things must change. The Lord has revealed to us that Christians have the opportunity to mightily influence the present as well as the future.

In Acts there is a moving story about two of Jesus' disciples, Peter and James. Tragically, James became the first of the twelve disciples to die a horrific death. It is my purpose to show you the difference fervent prayer can make in a person's life and what could be the result when it is absent.

James was a member of Jesus' innermost circle; you will recall there was Peter, James, and John. James and his brother John were given the name "Sons of Thunder" as a result of responding harshly to the Samaritans' rejection of Jesus (see Mark 3:17).

This apostle was privileged to accompany Jesus on special occasions. He saw more and experienced more than the other nine disciples. He was an eyewitness to the events that transpired on the Mount of Transfiguration. He actually saw Jesus talk to Moses and Elijah (see Matthew 17:3).

He was a significant player in the matrix of the early Church—a leading voice if you will. New believers looked to him for guidance and insight to their new life. He was able to share with them from an intimate perspective the teachings of Jesus. However, his life came to an abrupt and brutal end. No one within the Church thought that his incarceration would result in death. Perhaps a few days in jail, a public flogging, community humiliation, but not much more. They had watched their leaders be arrested and questioned before (see Acts 12:1).

However, this case was different. King Herod had had enough of the chaos being erected by Jesus' followers (see Acts 12:1).

> *Now about that time Herod the king stretched out his hand to harass some from the church. Then he killed James the brother of John with the sword* (Acts 12:1-2 NKJV).

Nervous shock waves traveled quickly through the early church when they received word that James, the disciple in Jesus' inner circle, was killed. No one fathomed such a thing could happen, especially to the beloved James.

FAST FORWARD

According to the biblical narrative, when King Herod saw how the death of James pleased the Jews, with haste he sought to kill the highest-ranking member of Jesus' group—Peter.

> *So when he had arrested him, he put him in prison, and delivered him to four squads of soldiers to keep him, intending to bring him before the people after Passover* (Acts 12:4 NKJV).

It is worth noting that Herod placed Peter in prison and surrounded him with sixteen soldiers. Their job was to watch and guard him closely and, no matter what, not to let him escape. Herod wanted to kill Peter just as he did James. He knew if he could kill him the event would propel him to unsurpassed popularity with the Jews, thus gaining him much-needed political influence. Meanwhile, the Church in Jerusalem was suffering in a multiplicity of ways due to James' untimely death. First, if James could be martyred, anyone could; second, most obviously, there was a giant vacuum in teaching and leadership. This void would have to be filled.

No One Prayed For James

When James was arrested by King Herod, it is interesting to note there is no record of the church praying for him. No doubt people were concerned, but the newly birthed church carried on business as usual—ministering to widows, Bible studies, community outreaches, etc. However, there is no mention of the church specifically gathering together to pray for divine intervention on behalf of the beloved disciple, James. The Bible says, *"Then he killed James the brother of John with the sword"* (Acts 12:2 NKJV).

The Church Shifted

The Church learned a valuable lesson from the death of James. The text below reveals their new strategy.

> *Peter was therefore kept in prison, but constant prayer was offered to God for him by the church* (Acts 12:5 NKJV).

This text soberly and yet subtly reveals what was missing when James was arrested—*prayer.* The Church was determined to not make the same mistake again; therefore, they regrouped and reconnected with the power of prevailing prayer.

One thing stands out in the verse above—*"constant prayer was offered."* This is quite interesting—not just prayer, but "constant prayer." Look how other translations describe what happened.

> *So Peter was kept in prison, but fervent and persistent prayer for him was being made to God by the church* (AMP).
>
> *While Peter was being kept in jail, the church never stopped praying to God for him* (CEV).
>
> *But while Peter was in prison, the church prayed very earnestly for him* (NLT).

What was the result of the church coming together and praying for Peter? The night before Herod was to bring Peter out to be questioned, Peter was soundly sleeping between two guards, bound by two chains. However, an angel entered his jail cell, woke him up, and escorted him to safety. Not one soldier knew Peter was gone until the next morning.

Peter had a dramatically different outcome than James; why? Everything was the same except one thing—constant and fervent prayer was made for Peter. God heard their cries and sent an angel to rescue him from certain death. It validates the truth that fervent and continual prayer changes impossible situations and events.

> **Fervent and continual prayer changes impossible situations and events.**

THE SECRET TO CONSTANT PRAYER

The Greek word used for "constant" prayer in Acts 12:5 is *ektenēs,* which denotes prayer that is ongoing, diligent, methodical, fiery, intentional, heartfelt, and passionate. This type of prayer moves men, governments, and even moves mountains; it is a threat to all spiritual strongholds, demonic powers, and political structures because it creates the atmosphere for the supernatural to occur.

The apostle Paul understood this realm of prayer and knew it wasn't your standard way of praying. It was more involved and required a greater focus and grit. On multiple occasions Paul called the church to the importance and expectation of laboring in prayer. Here is one example of a dear friend of the apostle Paul:

> *Epaphras, who is one of you, a bondservant of Christ, greets you, always laboring fervently for you in prayers, that you may stand perfect and complete in all the will of God* (Colossians 4:12 NKJV).

Again, Paul is denoting something significant here. The words "laboring fervently" come from the Greek word *agōnizomai.* The basic intent of this word denotes one is entering into a contest and competing for a prize. It also implies, "to contend with adversaries, fight, to struggle with difficulties and dangers."[3]

The very spelling of this word *agōnizomai* expresses "agonizing." It is the word from which our English word *agonize* is taken. It lends itself to more than routine praying or mouthing words to God out of formality, but carries a depth and weight of heart-wrenching, excruciating, harrowing prayer. This is another realm of prayer that many have never realized. I know many think that prayer should be sweet, simple, easy, and mild. And I agree at times it can be; however, we must remind ourselves we are engaged in a war for the souls of men and how we battle has eternal consequences.

To be involved in this realm of prayer, one has to put forth time and energy. This type of praying will not come easy. It will demand a lot from you, and afterward you will probably feel weary and perhaps even exhausted.

Becoming fully engaged in prayer physically, emotionally, and spiritually will be taxing on you. Because of the difficulty and discipline necessary for this type of praying, some will say it is too difficult and hard and they will want to quit. There is a common maxim that gives some excellent advice when we feel that way: "Pray hardest when it is hardest to pray."

I know this sentiment doesn't sit well with many in the body of Christ who have embraced the idea that everything should be free and easy. Some will frown upon even mentioning that we need to be physically engaged in releasing and executing the purposes of God on the earth. Regardless of contrary opinion, we cannot miss this specific call to prayer. Far too often we are too quick to retreat; we lose our stamina, our courage, or perhaps we get disappointed and back away or even stop pressing in to prayer due to being disheartened and frustrated with the lack of immediate results. Let us persevere and not quit.

Fervent praying is what gets results. We have to be relentless. This is the gold standard; this is how we ought to pray. Praying with fervency mixed with faith is what releases the angels of heaven and the power of His Kingdom upon the earth. There is no shortcut. Nothing else will do it— not our programs, not our preaching or worship, not even our holy desires. Only this kind of prayer prepares the way of the Lord!

> *Fervent praying is what gets results. We have to be relentless. This is the gold standard; this is how we ought to pray.*

WHAT DOES FERVENT PRAYER LOOK LIKE?

D.M. McIntyre reported before the great revival in Gallenkirchen broke out, Martin Boos spent hours and days and often nights in lonely agonies of intercession. Afterward, when he preached, "His words were as flame, and the hearts of the people as grass."[4] We have to recognize that the battle is not won simply by preaching; the battle is won in prayer.

To be fervent and earnest in prayer, one needs to identify emotionally and spiritually with the person or issue. They must feel impassioned about what they are praying for. Second, it has to be motivated by love with an equal resolve to be used of God to bring about the will of the Father to the people and situations we care so much about. Fervent praying involves a sense of urgency and desperation; the intercessor recognizes time is of the essence and will pray with that in mind.

CAN YOU IMAGINE THE POWER OF A HUNDRED PEOPLE PRAYING?

In order for us to see the extraordinary power of God dominating our churches, our lives, and our culture, we must enact extraordinary prayer. Our comfort level has to be disturbed; the way we have prayed in the past needs to be upgraded to a desperate level. Satan is on the prowl and his agenda has never been clearer. The body of Christ has to position themselves both offensively and defensively. I have discovered over the years that passionate and fervent prayer moves God. It touches His heart. He looks for it and quickly responds to it. God says so: *The effective, fervent prayer of a righteous man avails much*" (James 5:16).

Charles G. Finney talked about this type of praying:

I have never known a person sweat blood; but I have known a person pray till the blood started from his nose. And I have known persons to pray till they were all wet with perspiration, in the coldest weather in winter. I have known person pray for hours, till their strength was all exhausted with the agony of their minds. Such prayers prevailed with God.

If one person can move God by their tenacity, focus, and fervency, what could a group do? Furthermore, what type of Kingdom power and advancement could we accomplish if an entire church prayed together? If one person makes tremendous power available, what level of power could 100 believing saints make available? The devil knows the answer and trembles at the mere thought of it and works tirelessly to prevent it. He will let a church do almost anything except pray.

> **What type of Kingdom power and advancement could we accomplish if an entire church prayed together?**

This is why it is so difficult to get people to leave their homes, schedules, and other responsibilities to come and pray as a group. The gospel would spread more rapidly and have a deeper impact on those who embrace it, miracles would happen, strongholds would be broken off of people, revival would come, evangelists would preach without fear, churches would start to grow and new church plants would emerge, and thousands upon thousands of fire-baptized missionaries would be sent out to spread the gospel around the world.

Prayer is the number-one enemy of satan.

13

FINNEY AND FATHER NASH

We are weak in the pulpit be-
cause we are weak in the closet.
—JOHN ANGEL JAMES

Charles Grandison Finney struggled with his salvation experience. He wasn't convinced that he was truly saved. He committed himself to settle the question on whether or not he knew God. On October 10, 1821, he ventured into a patch of woods close to his home in Adams, New York. His purpose was to find God; he didn't want to live another day without the emphatic knowledge that Jesus was his Savior. He commented about his pursuit, "I will give my heart to God, or I never will come down from there." In a few hours he came back to his law office where he experienced such an encounter with the Lord that he doubted those who did not have a similar experience. He said of his encounter, "The Holy Spirit...seemed to go through me, body and soul. I could feel the impression, like a wave of electricity, going through and through me. Indeed it seemed to come in waves of liquid love, for I could not express it in any other way." The Lord changed the very core of Finney; he would never be the same. The next morning, Finney returned to his law office to meet with a client whose case he was about to argue. "I have a retainer from the Lord Jesus Christ to plead His cause," he told the man, "and cannot plead yours."

Finney resigned practicing law and began to evangelize. His ministry in the 1800s changed the spiritual landscape across America. Every church and minister felt the impact of his ministry. He was a key catalyst of the Second Great Awakening.

In fact, some historians call Finney the "father of modern revivalism." Plus, his ministry is said to have influenced and paved the way for great revivalists and evangelists like Dwight L. Moody, Billy Sunday, and Billy Graham. It is estimated that over 500,000 people responded to the invitation to come to Christ under Finney's ministry.[1]

HE HAD A TRUE FRIEND

Finney kept his personal affairs private. However, a newspaper reporter wanted to know why he was so persuasive and the secret to his power. It wasn't long until the reporter found the secret. He realized the source of Finney's power was the hours Finney spent in prayer.

> **The source of Finney's power was the hours Finney spent in prayer.**

It is also worth noting that when Finney was invited to speak, a friend named Daniel Nash would travel to the city three to four weeks ahead of him. Father Nash, as he became known, would find a suitable dwelling and begin to pray. After settling into the new town, Father Nash would try to gather a few others from the town who would agonize and intercede for God to move among the people. It was even discovered that Nash would rarely attend the revival services; he stayed hidden away seeking God to touch the hearts of the people while Finney ministered.

After arriving to a city in which Finney was to hold a revival meeting, a lady approached him with some concerns about Father Nash. Finney describes what she said:

> On one occasion when I got to town to start a revival a lady contacted me who ran a boarding house. She said, "Brother Finney, do you know a Father Nash? He and two other men have been at my boarding house for the last three days, but they haven't eaten a bite of food. I opened the door and peeped in at them because I could hear them groaning, and I saw them down on their faces. They have been this way for three days, lying prostrate on the floor and groaning. I thought something awful must have happened

to them. I was afraid to go in and I didn't know what to do. Would you please come see about them?" "No, it isn't necessary," Finney replied. "They just have a spirit of travail in prayer."[2]

This was Father Nash's ministry—to pray for Finney and the revival meetings. Finney described Father Nash's influence on his life this way:

> He would pray until he got an assurance in his mind that God would be with me in preaching, and sometimes he would pray himself ill. I have known the time when he has been in darkness for a season, while the people were gathering, and his mind was full of anxiety, and he would go again and again to pray, til finally he would come into the room with a placid face, and say: "The Lord has come, and He will be with us." And I do not know that I ever found him mistaken.[3]

Although he had a quiet demeanor, at times his prayers became loud and forceful. People recalled hearing him praying from behind closed doors—prayers would echo through the walls and could be heard from a distance, especially when he was praying for the unsaved. It is recorded that a man got saved when he heard Father Nash praying in a grove of trees.

Nash traveled with Finney for seven years, and it is recorded that the ministry of Finney had its greatest impact on society during the seven years while Father Nash interceded for him.

THEY WANTED TO HANG HIM!

Finney walked in a power that few had ever seen. For example, it was reported that one day as Charles Finney's train passed through Houghton, New York, the Holy Spirit fell on people in the town. Men who were in bars drinking and partying suddenly came under conviction and fell to their knees crying out for Jesus to save them.

Finney was a powerful force whom the devil and religious structure of his day feared. You would think a man who was turning entire cities upside down for the Lord would be supported by the ministry. Some of his greatest persecution came within the church. He never knew how he would be treated when he arrived in the town. Not all treated him unkindly, but many did. Below is a description of one such encounter—this was the town's greeting as he entered a town on his way to a revival meeting.

> Swinging above your heads are two distorted figures suspended on ropes. At the touch of the torch they leap into flames and the crowd screams in sheer delight. Sound like a scene from a lynching…a race riot? Not at all. It is a religious gathering. The charred creatures smoldering in the air represent the public's expression of opposition to the preaching and praying of

America's greatest evangelistic team. Charles Grandison Finney and his partner-in-prayer, Father Nash, have just been burned in effigy. Preachers and pew-warmers alike joined forces against the two men who did more to spearhead revival than any other pair in American history.[4]

Even though he experienced continuous attacks and religious vitriol, he persevered and remained true to his calling. He was bold and relentless and prepared the country for a mighty move of the Spirit. Even to this day the world is feeling the impact of Finney's ministry.

He Died Praying

In the winter of 1831, Father Nash was stricken with sickness. On December 20 of that year, while he was on his knees in prayer, he died at age 56. Below is what Finney said of his beloved friend:

> I have known that man go to bed absolutely sick, for weakness and faintness, under the pressure. And I have known him pray as if he would do violence to Heaven, and then have seen the blessing come as plainly in answer to his prayer as if it were revealed, so that no person could doubt it any more than if God had spoken from heaven.[5]

Finney added these thoughts:

Shall I tell you how he died? He prayed more and more; he used to take the map of the world before him, and pray, and look over the different countries and pray for them, till he expired in his room, praying. Blessed man! He was the reproach of the ungodly, and of carnal, unbelieving professors; but he was the favorite of Heaven, and a prevailing prince of prayer.[6]

|| 14 ||

"ARE Y'ALL POOR?"

Today, we are living in desperate times. Yet, the church is not desperate before God in prayer.
—CHUCK SMITH[1]

Beauty is in the eyes of the beholder—at least that is what they taught me.

Sometimes you have to rent before you buy. This is not bad; it is a part of life. I'll never forget—Karen and I were 19 and newly married. We were thrilled about our little house we were able to rent. To others it may not have meant much, but to us it was our home. It was off the main road down a step driveway tucked behind another house surrounded by unkempt bushes and trees. Nobody knew there was a house down there. The outside wasn't all that great—it badly needed to be painted, and kudzu vines had overtaken nearly the entire front of the house, growing wild. To me, it was extra insulation. Sometimes you have to look at the glass as half full. It had a dirt basement that I discovered to my surprise had snakes in it. Plus, there was little to no grass and the house was kind of smelly. Other than all of that, it was great! The positives were that we had running water, electricity, and a roof over our heads! We rented this house for an outrageous amount of $200 a month.

Karen and I made the best of the situation and worked hard to make it our home. However, the reality of our living condition was exposed by my nephew who came to visit us for the day. Two things happened—first, he survived the drive down our driveway; second, he got out of the car and looked at the house and then looked at Karen and the first words out of his mouth were, "Aunt Karen, are y'all poor?"

There is nothing like a reality check, and boy did we get it that day.

Currently, there are over 45 million rental households in the United States. Sometimes in the natural it is necessary to rent before you own your home. This is not bad. You rent until your hard work, discipline, and fiscal responsibility allow you to have enough money to purchase a home.

RENTING A MOVE OF GOD

We cannot buy the presence or the power of God. However, it is possible to rent a move of God for a few days. How do you rent a move of God? It's easy. As we discovered above, renting is cheaper than owning and the responsibilities are quite different as well. While renting you have very little responsibility other than a monthly rental fee. The owner is liable for major repairs and upkeep of the house.

Here is how church leadership can rent a move of God. You discover what type of movement you want in your church then you search for the person who carries that anointing—prophetic, evangelistic, healing, teaching, etc. You make a phone call and request if they are available to minister at your church. As advertised, the individual brings their anointing and without disappointing you have a great few services as the Lord's presence and power honor the gifting of the speaker and the faith of the people present. At the conclusion of the meetings, you give the minister an honorarium or love offering for their services and they eagerly move on to their next meeting. Typically after a few days the strong move of the Spirit at your church quickly dissipates, and in many cases your church returns to the way it was prior to the event.

Why? You rented a move of God.

Simon was used to seeing power. He was a sorcerer. For years he influenced the people of his community with his magic potions and spells. He recognized power when he saw it.

Simon witnessed the ministry of the apostle Paul and watched with his own eyes the strong impact the outpouring of the Holy Spirit was having on his friends and community. He wondered how he could have such power as the disciples. He was deeply intrigued.

Simon said, "What can I do to have this great power?" He wanted what they had and was willing to pay money for it. He wanted to pay for the gift and power of the Holy Spirit; however, God's economy doesn't work that way—He requires a different currency.

You have to pray the price in order to have power, revival, and glory.

> **You have to pray the price in order to have power, revival, and glory.**

A.T. Pierson (1837–1911), a magnificent missionary and theologian, made this observation:

> From the day of Pentecost, there has not been one great spiritual awakening in any land which has not begun in a union of prayer, though only among two or three; no such outward, upward movement has continued after such prayer meetings have declined.[2]

One thing is becoming more obvious—prayer is the key foundational pillar to seeing a sustained move of God. Extraordinary, united prayer is common to all revivals.

One of the great moves of God took place in Logan County, Kentucky—it is called the Cane Ridge Revival. This move started because people were concerned with the moral decline of the community and the utter coldness of believers.

God began to move. People flocked to the outdoor meetings at Cane Ridge desperate to hear a word from God and to experience His grace and power. The people gathered by the thousands (from 10,000 to 25,000). They would listen to messages that preachers in different places in those open fields would begin to preach.

One skeptic of the great outpouring who was later converted wrote:

> The noise was like the roar of Niagara. The vast sea of human beings seemed to be agitated as if by a storm. I counted seven ministers, all preaching at one time.... Some of the people were singing, others praying, some crying for mercy in the most piteous accents, while others were shouting most vociferously. While witnessing these scenes a peculiarly strange sensation, such as I had never felt before, came over me. My heart beat tumultuously, my knees trembled, my lip quivered, and I felt as though I must fall to the ground. A strange supernatural power seemed to pervade the entire the mass of mind there collected. ...At one time I saw at least five hundred swept down in a moment, as if a battery of a thousand guns had been opened upon them, and then immediately followed shrieks and shouts that rent the very heavens.[3]

Throughout the world, deep and substantial moves of God have led to major cultural shifts that have impacted the moral, spiritual, and political climates. Governments, churches, schools, and families have all had their immediate and future landscapes changed due to the heightened penetration of the glory and power of God.

|| 15 ||

IT STARTED WITH SIX

If the weight of His glory is your quest,
then prayer will be your priority.
—KIM OWENS

The moral decline in America is rapidly escalating, and we are entering into a period of unprecedented perversion, violence, and overall wickedness. No longer are moral values clear and basic laws upheld and seen as necessary. However, even as things continue to deteriorate I believe this is the perfect breeding ground for a move of God unlike the world has ever seen. Also, I am persuaded there is a remnant of God who are ready to do whatever it takes to see God move in our land.

I want to take you back to the time prior to the Third Great Awakening. The spiritual and moral climate was nearly non-existent. Here is a sample of what was happening in New York City in the late 1850s. As one researcher discovered:

One section of the city, noted for its bars and houses of ill fame, was called Satan's Circus. Any yokel who ventured there stood a good risk of getting jumped and robbed. Gangs would pour "knockout drops" into the drinks of unsuspecting saloon patrons, and then carry them out the door for a robbery, beating or worse.[1]

During this era a gang member was arrested and the police found in his pocked a price list for various acts of violence:

Punching	$2
Both eyes blacked	$4
Nose and jaw broken	$10
Ear chawed [sic] off	$15
Leg or arm broken	$19
Shot in leg	$25
"Doing the big job"	$100 and up[2]

In a message, a minister named Bishop Simpson made a bodacious statement. He said there were as many prostitutes as Methodists in New York City. He added that approximately one person in every 40 in the city was a prostitute.[3]

In June 1857 a newspaper reported about "The Great Police Riot." It took place in New York City Hall with rival police factions squaring off against one another. Fifty-three were injured.[4]

One month later "The Five Point Riots" took place in lower Manhattan over a new law to reduce alcohol consumption. Several were killed, and dozens were wounded.[5]

Then in August as chaos was on the increase, financial panic hit New York City. The oldest flour and grain company in New York failed. On its heels, the Ohio Life Insurance and Trust Company located in New York City suspended payments. Its failure led to a hysteria and panic on Wall Street and across America.[6]

THE THIRD GREAT AWAKENING

This awakening is known also as the "Layman's Prayer Revival." Even though it only lasted a few years, its impact is still being felt today.

Without question, as described above, the moral climate of New York City, and consequently the nation as a whole, was rapidly deteriorating. It was in this environment that a businessman decided to seek the heart and face of God. His name was Jeremiah Lanphier. Lanphier left his job as a businessman to be fully employed on July 1, 1857, as a City Missionary of the North Dutch Reformed Church on the corner of Fulton and William Streets. The church and its leadership grew gravely concerned about declining church attendance, as well as the spiritual condition of its neighbors in the Lower Manhattan area. Thus, Jeremiah Lanphier became their minister of evangelism. His job? Transform the community.

It didn't take long for Lanphier to realize that the area was spiritually destitute. Sinners and "Christians" alike were completely void of the life of God. Three months into his new ministry, he was gaining no new ground and his evangelistic progress was yielding little to no substantial fruit. However, he didn't quit. In fact, his burden was so great for his city that he began distributing pamphlets inviting people in the financial district to a weekly prayer meeting at noon at the North Dutch Church on Fulton Street. They gathered on the second floor of the church to pray for God to touch their lives and New York City.

Only six people showed for the first prayer gathering. However, the next week a few more inquiring souls joined them. Not to be discouraged, Jeremiah kept passing out pamphlets and personally inviting people to join him and the others for prayer.

In October, the people who had faithfully gathered together decided it was necessary to meet daily rather than weekly. God was moving, and within a few short weeks the number of people praying escalated and there was not enough room in the church to hold the noon prayer meeting. By the time winter settled in the Northeast, the Fulton Street Prayer Revival saw an expansion of the prayer meetings beyond the Dutch Church. Soon the Methodist Church on John Street and Trinity Episcopal Church on Broadway started holding daily prayer meetings. Other churches and meeting halls across the city began to open up at noon so people could pray. God was moving among His people.

According to the reports, as people gathered for prayer there was no fanaticism, hysteria, or emotionalism—only an impulse to pray. Charles Finney commented, "The general impression seemed to be, 'We have had instruction until we are hardened; it is now time for us to pray.'" In fact, there was very little preaching; those in attendance sat silent before the Lord. They sought His face and had an attitude of honoring and glorifying Him.[7]

As a result of people seeking God, the Lord's Spirit began swirling over the city, and a profound sense of the fear of God was everywhere. For example, chronic criminals started turning themselves in to the police. It was reported that in one of the prayer gatherings a person who planned to commit murder and then to commit suicide, confessed his plans to the group. The power of God was gripping the hearts of those present in the meetings as well as those outside.

Again, the presence of God due to the prayer meetings was pervasive and persistent upon the hearts of nearly every person in the city. The entire city was being impacted by the manifest presence of God. And it wasn't limited to the land either. It was reported that even ships that were entering into the harbor in New York City felt the inescapable presence of God hovering on and around the perimeter of the city— the passengers aboard fell under irresistible conviction and began to repent of their sin and turn to God.

More Than 6,000 People!

A very energetic newspaper reporter from the *New York Times* used his horse and buggy and galloped through town to observe as many prayer meetings as possible in order to get a count of the participants. He made it to ten prayer meetings and counted 6,110 people in attendance.[8]

Multitudes were getting born again at the prayer gatherings. In May 1858, the Presbyterian magazine projected that 50,000 New Yorkers had entered the Kingdom of God in the first five months of 1858.

The move of God was so important and widespread that many local business owners closed their stores so they and their employees could join the prayer effort.

Charles Finney, who was responsible for Lanphier's conversion, was making his way from Nebraska to Boston to minister and he said, "Prayer meetings dotted the entire 2,000 miles."[9] This move of God happened because one simple man knew the only way to save a city wasn't through more programs but by prayer.

God's conditions must be met.

Here is what we must embrace—God desires to save and rescue His people; however, for that to happen God's conditions must be met. I am convinced God will hear us if we pray. His face can be found if we seek it. And He will approach us if we humbly approach Him. In essence,

without fail God will heal us and our land if we humble ourselves, pray, seek His face, and turn from our wicked ways
(see 2 Chronicles 7:14).

|| SECTION 4 ||

UNLESS WE WAR

|| 16 ||

URGENCY

You know the value of prayer: it is precious
beyond all price. Never, never neglect it.
—SIR THOMAS BUXTON

H ave you ever felt the need for urgency? Perhaps when you are running late to an important meeting, or family and friends are coming over and the house isn't clean and the food isn't prepared? Or you are on a basketball team and you are behind and the seconds are ticking off the clock? If so, you know the definition of urgency. When urgency is needed things speed up, focus becomes narrowed, things become prioritized, and every second matters. The word *urgent* comes from an old Latin word meaning "to urge." It means that an event is occurring that is so compelling it requires immediate attention and action.

At the height of tension and racial unrest in America, Dr. Martin Luther King, Jr. was scheduled to speak at a massive rally on August 28, 1963. People from all over America marched on the nation's capital—250,000 were in attendance. They came to protest and to hear numerous national leaders speak on racial inequality. Dr. King was the last speaker of the day, at 3:00 p.m., and was scheduled to only speak for four minutes. The scene was beautifully orchestrated—his back was to a sacred memorial dedicated to the 16th president of the United States, Abraham Lincoln, who signed the Emancipation Proclamation nearly 100 years earlier. In front of him were thousands of hopeful faces looking for justice and equality. They came to hear words of hope, and they were not disappointed. Dr. King delivered the famous "I Have a Dream" speech.

Dr. King went well beyond the four minutes allocated and spoke for sixteen minutes. Every word was draped with conviction, fervency, and passion. One of his most famous lines came four and a half minutes into his address. Dr. King said, "We have come to this hallowed spot to remind America of the fierce urgency of now."

History affirms the gravity of this speech, and many feel it was one of the most pivotal moments in the civil rights movement. Those sixteen minutes captivated and influenced the heart of the American public. It shook the nation. The message clearly communicated, "We must have action, and something needs to be done now." Historians believe the march and especially this speech was the catalyst for the signing of the Civil Rights Act of 1964 and the Voting Rights Act of 1965.

Dr. King pushed for an immediate responsive action to meet the level of urgency surrounding the injustice black people were experiencing. Stagnation was no longer a viable option. Because of Dr. King's resolve and relentless messaging, the course of America was forever changed.

Being Willing Is Not Enough

Once again, urgency is defined this way: "importance requiring swift and immediate action, insistence." When something is urgent, complacency is not an acceptable course of action.

Leonardo da Vinci, the Italian Renaissance painter who created the "Mona Lisa" and "The Last Supper," is supposed to have said, "I have been impressed with the urgency of doing. Knowing is not enough; we must apply. Being willing is not enough; we must do."

What was da Vinci saying to us? For starters, he was reminding us all that just "knowing" that something needs to be done is not enough—there must be action that supports our revelation. Something physically needs to be done.

> *There must be action that supports our revelation.*

This applies to each of us when it comes to prayer. We know we need to pray, but that is not enough—we must pray. We no longer can kick the can down the road and promise to do better tomorrow. The clock is ticking and time is of the essence. Later may be too late and tomorrow may never come. Three words need to be added to our life—*urgent, now,* and *today.*

The Night Is Coming

In John 9, in the midst of healing a blind man Jesus made the statement, *"I must work the works of Him who sent Me while it is day; the night is coming when no one can work"* (John 9:4).

The words of Jesus in verse 4 should startle us all. He said there is *a time coming when no man can work.*

The "night" in the text is not talking about just the absence of physical light but a specific span or period of time. It cannot be taken for granted that Jesus, in the midst of a man receiving sight, chose to teach us an eternal principle. He was highlighting the uniqueness and brevity of opportunity and the preciousness of time, indicating that each moment we have been allotted should not be squandered or mishandled. We must realize that when our opportunity/time expires, what has been done cannot be reversed, corrected, or amended. So the moment to act and do is now.

The tower at George W. Truett Seminary in Waco, Texas, is home to a larger-than-life clock. Right below the clock these piercing words are inscribed: "THE NIGHT COMETH."

When people view the clock to see what time it is, their eyes are drawn to Jesus' words, "the night cometh." These three simple words remind the seminary students and all who pass by that the night is fast coming and that time is passing. They are admonished in a not so subtle way that every minute matters and every opportunity must be seized in order to assist the cause of Christ around the world.

As we all know quite well, time is always moving. It is unstoppable. You can't halt its advancement. A young person looks at time as if it is slowly crawling, but to the aged, time speeds forward like a race car that gets faster with every lap. Nonetheless, for both it is advancing like a determined army. It slips away day by day, hour by hour, minute by minute, and second by second. You can't bank time, store it up, and use it later—it doesn't work that way.

> You can't bank time, store it up, and use it later—it doesn't work that way.

This message of Jesus was so impacting and profound that the Scottish preacher Robert Murray M'Cheyne, on the dial of his watch, had drawn a picture of the setting sun, and underneath were the words of this verse, "for the night cometh." This reminded him of the urgency of the task at hand and that night was approaching when he could no longer work for his Savior. As one pastor said:

> The call of scripture is ever and always one of urgency. Every page of the Bible says "today." Every tick of the clock says "today." Every beat

of your heart says "today." Every obituary column
in the newspaper says "today."[1]

Time is precious, most precious. Why? Because it is limited; there isn't an endless supply of it. It's not renewable. Don't let that depress you, but let it motivate you to get busy. The clock is ticking—don't let another day pass without fervently praying. There is a lot at stake. You alone hold the keys to the Kingdom over your life and surroundings. Embrace this challenge because night cometh!

It was said of Wales in 1904 that you knew revival was on the way when you heard the "Oh" of desperation and urgency in the prayers.

Again, urgency is the opposite of satisfaction and complacency. We are living in dangerous times; the hour is late and we cannot afford to drift aimlessly with no purpose or plan. It isn't enough for us to talk about prayer; we must do it. Martyn Lloyd-Jones said that in movements of the Spirit:

> Generally the very first thing that happens, and
> which eventually leads to a great revival, is that
> one man, or a group of men, suddenly begin to
> feel this burden, and they feel the burden so
> much that they are led to do something about it.[2]

Jonathan Edwards, who was instrumental and a catalyst in the First Great Awakening, said, "When God has something to accomplish for His church, it is with His will that there should precede it the extraordinary prayer of

His people." Every time this happens, believing prayer dislodges the rigidity of the old ways, old traditions, and old strongholds. Prayer pushes the staleness and coldness off of the church and its members. Prayer is like a weather front moving in—it drives the stalled religious systems out of the way and makes room for His glory and power.

|| 17 ||

MOBILIZED FOR WAR

Blessed be the Lord, my rock, who trains my
hands for war, and my fingers for battle.
—PSALM 144:1 ESV

My mother-in-law once said to her daughter, to whom I am now married, "Those who don't listen have to feel."

Here is the interpretation of this nugget of parental wisdom. If you listen and follow the instructions, all is well and you will be happy and prosperous. However, if you want to venture out and ignore the parameters of behavior, you will suffer the consequences. This is how this principle works—for example, "Don't touch the stove." Well, you know that every child who hears those words immediately wants to touch the stove. Their adventurous minds want to know what they are missing out on. And when they don't obey and stretch their bony finger to touch the stove, they will immediately feel the impact fire has on the human body—*pain!* Reiterating this pearl of discernment: "Those who don't listen have to feel."

I experienced the reality of this truth more than I would like to admit. Because I wanted to do things my way, I usually had to feel on my backside the pain of a perfectly selected switch from the shrubs adorning the front of my house. If knowing I was about to be the recipient of multiply slashes wasn't enough torment, my mom made me go get the switch for her. The walk there was brutal. Once in front of the bush, I wanted to select the branch I thought would inflict the least amount of pain. After you have been through this regimen, you kind of know which ones hurt more than others, so you choose wisely. On my return with switch in hand, my mom would take it and look at it as if to inspect it, making sure it had a certain elasticity so it could accomplish its brutal, intended purpose upon my person. Because I often didn't listen, I had to feel, and believe me I felt a lot of pain.

The Church at large has not fully embraced Jesus' model of ministry, and in many cases we have watered down the message in order to be more appealing to the unreached. I am afraid that we now find ourselves feeling the pain of losing a culture, society, and nation. We are seeing the devastating results of cutting corners in order to draw bigger crowds.

I am not trying to be judgmental or overly critical; I am simply making an observation of not only my ministry but others' as well.

It seems we have tried to do it our way. We have put our hope in people, programs, ministries, giftings, meetings, worship, conferences, and even our good preaching. All of the above are good and noble expressions, but these alone haven't improved the spiritual climate of our churches or our nation. Maybe when we run out of physical energy and have exhausted all other means, we once again will depend on the one thing that brings God to our churches—prayer.

> *Maybe when we run out of physical energy and have exhausted all other means, we once again will depend on the one thing that brings God to our churches—prayer.*

The now-deceased, world-renowned evangelist R.A. Torrey said, "I have a theory...that there is not a church, chapel, or mission on earth where you cannot have revival, provided there is a little nucleus of faithful people who will hold onto God until He comes down."

Isn't this good news? John G. Lake was a world-renowned evangelist in the early years of the 20th century. His ministry was marked with prayerfulness and remarkable divine demonstrations. Newspapers across the country reported on the exploits and miracles that were taking place during his meetings.

Lake once told the story of an angel who appeared to him while he read the book of Acts. Lake said the angel pointed him to each time the Spirit of God was poured out in the early church, and each outpouring was preceded by a season of seeking God's face.

The angel then told Lake: "This is Pentecost as God gave it through the heart of Jesus. Strive for this. Contend for this. Teach people to pray for this. For this, and this alone, will meet the necessity of the human heart, And this alone will have the power to overcome the forces of darkness."

Before the angel left Lake, he said one final thing: "Pray. Pray. Pray. Teach the people to pray. Prayer and prayer alone, much prayer, persistent prayer, Is the door of entrance into the heart of God."[1]

Satan's Highest Priority

Satan's greatest work and highest priority is to cause a slumber across the body of Christ that keeps us unaware of and disinterested in effectual corporate prayer. This is his highest priority. Without question, the domain of darkness trembles when God's people pray, and the demons of hell will do whatever is necessary to keep us from praying. Therefore, every prayer initiative has a counter initiative. Whenever believers pray within the will of God—in other words, contend with clarity for God's will to be done— satan and the powers of hell are aware of their efforts and seek to delay or deter God's intervention. Prayer is work and takes disciplined focus in order to accomplish God's will on the earth.

Again, not meaning to sound redundant but the devil knows that prayer is the catalyst that advances the Kingdom of God. Prayers are not meant to only be reactionary or defensive—in other words, "Let's pray because something bad has happened." There are times we pray in response to something, but prayer needs to be used as an offensive weapon that clears the way for the Lord to move ahead. Please understand, when we pray, the Kingdom aggressively storms forward.

> **When we pray, the Kingdom aggressively storms forward.**

GOD IS WAITING

There isn't a new way or new thing God is going to do to move His Kingdom forward. He set the pattern in place long ago, and it has not changed. The Church has many functions, but its primary function is to pray. The bedrock of the Church was set into place by Jesus when He said, "*My house shall be called a house of prayer for all the nations*" (Mark 11:17 ESV). Notice, it is "a house" of prayer, which doesn't only indicate a building that has a designated purpose, but the emphasis is on the latter part of the phrase, a house "of" prayer. In other words, this is what this house does—it prays.

The message could not be clearer. God waits on His people to pray. It is His desire, His way. The first church was birthed as a result of prayer (see Acts 1–2), and it continued to demonstrate the power of the Spirit because of prayer. One hundred twenty believers filled with the Holy Spirit and empowered through prayer turned the world upside down. This is our example, our pattern.

Sound of the Bugle

During India's mutiny against Great Britain in 1857-58, British soldiers were camped outside the city of Delhi when the British commander gave the order for his men to attack the city. Medical personnel began to move among the troops to determine who among them was fit for battle. A young soldier lay wounded, and as the medic looked at him, he pleaded, "Sir, please don't declare me unfit for battle. It's just a fever, and the sound of the bugle will make me well."

This is a great example of the courage and strength needed in this hour. The soldier's thoughts were not on his own plight but the war at hand, his duty, and his responsibility. Believers have to come to the understanding that this war has eternal consequences. A paradigm shift is needed, and we have to make the transition in our spirits that no longer is it about my "needs," my "breakthrough," my "touch," or my "blessing." We no longer make it about, "What can God do for me?" The conclusion must be reached, "What do I need to do to be used of God in order to fight this spiritual battle in order to rescue the perishing around me?"

The bugle has sounded! We are at war, and we must pay whatever price in order to advance the cause of Christ. It has been said, "Our gentle prayers accomplish so little, but then they cost us so little." May this never be said of this generation of believers.

|| 18 ||

VIOLENT PRAYING

*The man who mobilizes the Christian church
to pray will make the greatest contribu-
tion to world evangelization in history.*
—ANDREW MURRAY

A young football coach was hired as a scout or recruiter for
his college. Before his first assignment, he said, "Coach,
what kind of player are you looking for?"

The coach said, "Well, there is a kind of guy who, when
you knock him down, just stays down."

The recruiter asked, "We don't want him, do we, Coach?"

"No." Then the coach said to the recruiter, "There is the
kind of guy who, when you knock him down, he gets up;
knock him down again, he gets back up; if you knock him
down another time, he gets back up; knock him down and
he gets up—every time!"

"That's the guy we want! Right, Coach?"

"No, we don't want him either. What I want you to find is the guy who is knocking all the other guys down. That's the guy I want."

In this desperate hour God is like the coach—find me the guy who is knocking all the other guys down. Samuel Chadwick once said, "There are blessings of the Kingdom that are only yielded to the violence of the vehement soul."[1] There is a new attitude entering the Church. We can no longer be passive or casual about our prayer life. We have to change our approach to prayer. There are times we need to become violent in the spirit—be willing to knock some things down.

> **There are times we need to become violent in the spirit—be willing to knock some things down.**

Violent praying means there is a level of fervency and tenacity coming from the depths of someone's heart due to the anguish they see and feel. It is a soul that is in spiritual and, oftentimes, a physical agony over the unbridled misery in society. This type of praying is effectual—why? The one doing the praying emphatically knows what the will of God is and demands that it be done. People who understand this level of praying persevere until the battle is won. I have discovered, historically and biblically, that violent praying moves mountains and shakes kingdoms and melts hearts. Heaven, hell, and the earth all feel the reverberations of prayer that is expressed from a determined, relentless, strong-willed prayer warrior. Satan fears this type of praying person the most.

THE PLACE SHOOK

Duncan Campbell, who was the leading figure in the Hebrides Revival (1949), shared a story of what fervent and violent prayer looks like. These are his words:

> I think one of the most outstanding things that happened I believe will go down in history as long as revival is mentioned was in the parish of Arnot. Now, I regret to say that here I was bitterly opposed by a certain section of the Christian church. ...They were so successful in their opposition that very few people from this particular community came near any of my meetings.
>
> ...So one night one of the elders came to me and said, "Mr. Campbell, there is only one thing that we can do. We must give ourselves to prayer— give ourselves to prayer. Prayer changes things." "Well you know I am very willing for that," I said. "Where will we meet?" "Oh," he said, "There is a farmer and he is very willing to place his farmhouse at our disposal." It was winter and the church was cold. There was no heating in it. The people believe in a crowded church

to provide its own heat. But here we wanted a warmer spot, and the farmer was approached. Now the farmer wasn't a Christian nor his wife but they were God-fearing.

…Men who had burdens—longings to see God move in revival. And we were praying and oh, the going was hard. At least I felt it hard. It came to between 12 or 1 o'clock in the morning when I turned again to this blacksmith whom I have already referred to. Oh, he was a prince in the parish. And I said to him, "John, I feel that God would have me to call upon you to pray." Up until then he was silent. And that dear man began—he must have prayed for about a half an hour. When he paused for a second or so and then looking up towards the heavens he cried, "God, do You know that Your honor is at stake? Do You know that Your honor is at stake? You promised to pour water on the thirsty and floods on the dry ground and, God, You are not doing it." Now my dear people, could we pray like that? Ah, but here was a man who could. Here was a man who could. He then he went on to say, "There are five ministers in this meeting and I don't know where a one of them stands in Your presence, not even Mr. Campbell." Oh, he was an honest man. "But if I know anything at all about my own poor heart, I think I can say and I think that You know that I'm thirsty! I'm thirsty to see the devil defeated in this parish. I'm thirsty to see this community gripped as You gripped Barvas. I'm longing for revival and God, You are not doing it! I am thirsty and You promised to pour water on me." Then a pause and then he cried, "God, I now take upon myself to challenge You to fulfil Your covenant engagement!" Now it was nearing two o'clock in the morning.

What happened? The house shook. A jug on a sideboard fell onto the floor and broke. A minister beside me said, "An earth tremor." And I said, "Yes." But I had my own thoughts. My mind went back to Acts chapter 4 when they prayed the place was shaken. When John Smith stopped praying at twenty minutes past two, I pronounced the benediction and left the house. What did I see? The whole community alive. Men carrying chairs, women carrying stools and asking, "Is there room for us in the churches?" And the Arnol revival broke out. And oh, what a sweeping revival! I don't believe there was a single house in the village that wasn't shaken by God. I went into another farmhouse—I was thirsty, I was tired, I needed something to drink. And I went into ask for a drink of milk and

I found nine women in the kitchen crying to God for mercy—nine of them! The power of God swept—and here was a little boy. Oh, he's kneeling by a pigsty and he is crying to God for mercy. And one of the elders goes over to him and prays over him and little Donald MacPhail came to know the Savior and I believe more souls were brought to Christ through that one lad's prayers than through the preaching of all of the ministers from the island, me included. God used him. He was the boy that prayed, "I gazed upon an open door."

Now that night do you know that the drinking house was closed. Now that's a way back—1952—and it has never been opened since. I was back some time ago and an old man pointed at this house with its windows boarded up and he said, "Mr. Campbell, do you see that house over there? That was the drinking house of the past. Do you know that last week at our prayer meeting 14 of the men who drank there were praying men." Now, people—that's revival. That is God at work. Miracles, supernatural, beyond human explanation—it's God.[2]

Campbell shared another story of the power of prayer. A group of people gathered in Barvas to fervently pray for a neighboring village that was resistant to the revival that was taking place. The people of the village disdained what God was doing and opposed it every way they could. While the group prayed:

> A schoolmaster that night looking over his papers 15 miles away from this island on the mainland suddenly was gripped by the fear of God. And he said to his wife, "Wife, I don't know what's drawing me to Barvas, but I must go." His wife said, "But it's nearly 10 o'clock and you're thinking of going to Barvas. I know what's on your mind, I know that you are going out to drink and you are not leaving this house tonight!" That was what she said to him—he was a hard drinker. And he said to his wife, "I may be mistaken, oh, I maybe mistaken, but if I know anything at all about my own heart and mind, I think I say to you now that drink will never touch my lips again." And she said to him, "Well, John, if that's your mind, then go to Barvas." And he got someone to take him to the ferry, someone to ferry him across, and I [Duncan Campbell] was conducting a meeting in a farmhouse at midnight and this schoolmaster came to the door and they made room for him and in a matter of minutes he was praising God for salvation. Now that's miracle. I mean you cannot explain it in any other way.[3]

In the midst of a revival in 1859 in Wales, nearly a half a century before the famous Welsh Revival, a reporter for a church magazine reported how sinners were responding to God's conviction as a result of fervent and violent praying from a group of concerned Christians. He said:

> I have never witnessed anything like that which I now see daily. You hear of nothing but the revival. Ungodly people quake and tremble... I have seen a large congregation in this neighborhood, containing at the time many scores of hardened ungodly people, bathed in tears, and as incapable of leaving the place at the close of the public service as if their feet had been nailed to the floor of the chapel... Some of the most ungodly men seemed to be entirely bewildered; they could hardly find their way home that night. Blessed be God! Many of them found their way to the blood of the Cross. ...God in His grace, has done more within the past two weeks in this part of the country than had been accomplished for an age previously.[4]

Violent praying can and should involve your entire physical makeup, not just your mind. Violent praying can become emotional as your body becomes fully engaged in when you are at war during intercession. Our emotions when controlled can lead us into powerful times of intercession. Don't neglect this side of your physical makeup. It was placed in you by God.

19

CRITICAL 11 MINUTES

*Prayer is the way you defeat the devil, reach the
lost, restore the backslider, strengthen the saints,
send missionaries out, cure the sick, accomplish
the impossible, and know the will of God.*
—DAVID JEREMIAH

I had the privilege of sitting next to a seasoned Delta Airlines
pilot on a return flight to Atlanta. Needless to say, I wanted
to know everything about flying a plane. I was intrigued by
his vast understanding of airplanes and his attention to the
safety and wellbeing of the passengers under his care. I was
curious and wanted to know, "What is the most important
part of flying an airplane?"

He didn't hesitate to answer. He looked at me and said
with a serious tone, "It is what is called the critical eleven
minutes." He added, "The first eight minutes when you are
leaving the ground as the plane begins to climb are crucial.

And then the last three minutes as a plane is descending to land are equally important." He paused afterward as if to meditate on the severity of those precious eleven minutes. The truth about the eleven minutes obviously had been drilled into him by his instructors and every time he stepped into the flight simulator.

I will never forget what he said about the critical eleven minutes of a flight! I find it interesting that he highlighted the beginning of the flight and the ending as the most important.

> *Our attention and commitment to prayer must not wane as we look for His return, for we have much work to do.*

How true this is for the Church today! In Acts 2, the Church was born with an explosion of power that remained a part of the New Testament Church for centuries. The Church had to be birthed and launched forward in this fashion. It had to break through the religious gravitational pull of that time. And due to the thrust of the Holy Spirit, the Church "took off," and for two thousand years we have been walking in that power. However, I believe the Lord is about to land the plane. The end of time is approaching— we are in the last critical three minutes. How we navigate these last days is crucial. We cannot coast to the end. Our ending is just as important as our beginning. Our attention and commitment to prayer must not wane as we look for His return, for we have much work to do.

In fact, as airplanes descend to their destination and are met with turbulence, so shall it be with the Church. However, due to our attention to prayer and walking in Kingdom power, we will finish strong!

What Is Needed?

In order to finish like we started, we have to have a paradigm shift; prayer can no longer be viewed as a luxury but a necessity. We need praying men and women like John Hyde. John, who at times was called the "Apostle of Prayer," had a tenacious praying spirit. He was a young man when he traveled to India to be a missionary. Over the years while there, he developed and grew into a disciplined prayer warrior. With each passing season, his prayer life continued to grow, flourish, and strengthen. It was reported that Hyde agonized, travailed in prayer four hours a day. This helped him lead to Christ at least four Indian souls a day while he was in India.

After years of ministry, Hyde became seriously ill. He quickly visited a doctor and a thorough physical exam was given. The doctor said, "Mr. Hyde, what are you doing to yourself? What unusual stress, strain, and agony are you submitting to? Your physical heart is in the worst condition I have ever seen. It has actually moved in your chest cavity. What are you doing?"

The answer? He had completely given himself to prayer. He knew if the nation of India was to be saved it wouldn't happen by preaching alone. Prayer was the key.

When John Hyde passed, the eulogies poured in, but they were not sent to his common name, John Hyde. They were addressed to a different name, Praying Hyde, the name by which the locals in India called him. They knew their nation was moved toward Jesus because of the time Hyde spent in agonizing prayer for them.

I Heard Him Pray

The fiery evangelist D.L. Moody visited Spurgeon's church, and when asked did he get to hear Spurgeon preach, he responded, "Yes, but better still I heard him pray." Spurgeon understood the enormity of a praying people. In one of his published sermons he wrote, "Shall I give you yet another reason why you should pray? I have preached my very heart out. I could not say any more than I have said. Will not your prayers accomplish that which my preaching fails to do? Is it not likely that the church has been putting forth its preaching hand but not its praying hand? Oh dear friends, let us agonize in prayer."[1]

The biggest task God has for the modern Church is to get us to pray. Usually without hesitation we gather to worship, we gather to hear good preaching, we even pay good money to attend conferences, but we have relatively few who gather to pray. In these last days the Church must realize the critical hour we are in and respond accordingly.

> **The biggest task God has for the modern Church is to get us to pray.**

The early disciples understood the necessity of prayer in their personal lives and ministry. They diligently guarded this segment of their life. When the first church exploded in numbers, a well-meaning group within the church came to the disciples and requested that they become more visible, approachable, and help serve those in need and particularly the widows. The apostles quickly addressed their worries, "*It is not desirable that we should leave the word of God and serve tables*" (Acts 6:2 NKJV).

Again, Peter heard their concerns and validated his priorities, "*we will give ourselves continually to prayer and to the ministry of the word*" (Acts 6:4 NKJV).

Note: The widows and their needs were valid and needed attention, but Peter made it clear to all that nothing was more important to him than prayer. Prayer was the early disciples' highest priority; in fact, they "gave" themselves to it. Prayer was their life, their calling—it was essential. They knew if they were to represent Christ and demonstrate the power of the Holy Spirit, prayer had to hold the paramount position in their life.

Peter's mindset reminds me of Nehemiah when he was rebuilding the walls of Jerusalem. Two men wanted to meet with Nehemiah to discuss their concerns regarding the wall. Four times they entreated him to come off the wall to meet with them. Nehemiah knew this was a distraction that would greatly affect the rebuilding of the walls of Jerusalem. Each time they approached him, he responded with the same answer:

> *I am doing a great work, so that I cannot come down. Why should the work cease while I leave it and go down to you?* (Nehemiah 6:3 NKJV)

Nehemiah called what he was doing a "great work." What if we treated prayer as the great work it is and refused to come down for any reason from our place of intercession? These last few days and minutes we have left need our full devotion to prayer. It is critical!

|| SECTION 5 ||

UNLESS WE GATHER

20

THE CINDERELLA
OF THE CHURCH

*The devil will try to stop you from pray-
ing because prayer stops him.*
—REINHARD BONNKE

By now you have learned every significant revival that has
marked the earth had a similar beginning. *Prayer!* You
can't wish or work to make revival happen. True revival is
more than a three-day meeting you put on a calendar. Tens
of thousands of such meetings occur in America each year.
Though I am grateful for all the fruit that comes from them,
we are no closer to an awakening. Why? Perhaps they lacked
sustained prayer. Edwin Orr said, "History is silent about
revivals that did not begin with prayer."

I learned the hard way—you can't buy revival, nor can
you preach or even worship it into existence. Revival comes
forth from great travail and a life laid down, only after it

passes through the womb of intercession. This only happens when an individual or group of believers sets their heart to pray and labor for it until it comes. This pursuit is difficult; it has many obstacles. It takes resilient effort, humility, and persistence. However, the effort is worth it and the kingdom of darkness feels it.

The soul of every move of God is prayer, especially corporate prayer. The devil knows this and tries to prevent it at every stage. When the Church organizes to pray, the enemy brings unbelievable resistance on many levels. Why? He knows when we pray the heavens move and the domain of darkness is greatly impacted.

Prayer is like a stick of dynamite in God's hands. When we pray in accordance with God's will, He releases His will accompanied with power that obliterates spiritual barriers, destroys demonic opposition, and obstacles of all sorts are removed.

BLOOD IN HIS SHOES

The late Dr. Paul Yonggi Cho pastored the largest church in the world in Seoul, South Korea. He said, "There is one great difference in the Church in America and the Church in Korea. The Church in America has very much program and little prayer; the Church in Korea has very much prayer and little program."[1]

In the first three years of pastoring, Dr. Cho recalled that he did not go to his apartment for a three-year period. He slept, wept, and prayed in his church. He said of that time, "Many times my body would be so weakened from fasting that when I stood to preach, blood would seep from my legs and feet and fill my shoes."[2] He knew the hour demanded more than mere words and action—it required prayer, much prayer.

Passivity and indifference must be replaced with awareness of the hour and an urgency that equals the mission before us.

> **Passivity and indifference must be replaced with awareness of the hour and an urgency that equals the mission before us.**

Dr. Cho's admonition reminds me of the words of Edward Payson, "Prayer is the first thing, the second thing, and the third thing necessary for a minister, especially in seasons of revival. Pray then, my dear brother, pray, pray, pray."[3]

It is hard to build momentum for prayer with the church congregation when it isn't scheduled. I have discovered that corporate prayer will gain a more prominent place within the ministry of the church when it is fixed on the calendar, immovable, and enthusiastically promoted and attended by the leadership. Caution: if the lead pastors and senior leadership do not attend the prayer meetings, the prayer ministry of the church will never take root in the congregation. Corporate prayer has to be what a church does continually, not just when there is a big event a few days away.

Pensacola Outpouring

Steve Strang of *Charisma News* conducted an insightful interview with Pastor John Kilpatrick, who led the great Brownsville Revival (1995–2001). Over 4 million people came from around the world to Brownsville Assembly of God in Pensacola, Florida, to experience the revival fire. The following is an excerpt of that interview.

[Pastor Kilpatrick] still remembers the incredible way God stirred it up—and it all started with prayer.

"Prayer is what sparked it," he says. "God never puts revival on sale. It'll cost this generation, but it cost previous generations. ...The Lord spoke to me, and He said, 'If you'll make this a house of prayer, I'll pour out My Spirit here.'"

When Kilpatrick received that word, he began holding a prayer meeting every Sunday night. The Lord told him to set up 12 prayer banners that represented 12 categories to pray for. People would go from banner to banner, praying for each topic and getting so excited about prayer that meetings soon began lasting around two hours or longer.

Kilpatrick and his church prayed faithfully like this for [two and a half years] before revival broke out. For about the first year of that time,

Kilpatrick would hear a voice accusing him each week, telling him to stop these prayer meetings, or he would lose his followers.

"As we were praying, I heard the Holy Spirit speak," he tells me. "And He said, 'You have held tight. Now I'm about to send forth My Spirit in this place in a mighty way.'"

As soon as Kilpatrick heard that prophetic word, the accusing voice went silent, and he never heard it again. Revival swept through that church a year and a half later in 1995.[4]

The Pensacola Outpouring began like all other revivals—with corporate prayer. E.M. Bounds wrote regarding the beauty of a praying church, "A praying church is stronger than all the gates of hell." Certainly, the gates of hell felt the full brunt of the prayers of the believers at the Brownsville Assembly of God as thousands were gloriously saved, healed, and empowered. Leonard Ravenhill said:

> The Cinderella of the church of today is the prayer meeting. This handmaid of the Lord is unloved and unwooed because she is not dripping with the pearls of intellectualism, nor glamorous with the silks of philosophy; neither is she enchanting with the tiara of psychology. She wears the homespuns of sincerity and humility and so is not afraid to kneel![5]

Ravenhill added, "The law of prayer is the law of harvest: sow sparingly in prayer, reap sparingly; sow bountifully in prayer, reap bountifully. The trouble is we are trying to get from our efforts what we never put into them."[6]

> The corporate praying meeting must be restored to the church. If your church doesn't have one, you must work diligently to start it.

Charles Spurgeon tells a funny story of how one lady refused to stop going to church to pray even though the church "prayer meeting" had been permanently cancelled. He said:

> Be like the good woman who, when it was decided to close the prayer-meeting in a certain village, declared that it should not be, for she would be there if no one else was. She was true to her word; and when, the next morning, someone said to her rather jestingly, "Did you have a prayer-meeting last night?" "Ah, that we did!" she replied. "How many were present?" "Four," she said. "Why," said he, "I heard that you were there all alone." "No," she said, "I was the only one visible, but the Father was there, and the Son was there, and the Holy Spirit was there, and we were agreed in prayer." Before long, others took shame to themselves at the

earnest perseverance of a poor old woman, and soon there was a revived prayer-meeting and a prospering church.[7]

Spurgeon also said, "Brethren, we shall never see much change for the better in our churches in general till the prayer-meeting occupies a higher place in the esteem of Christians."[8]

A Kingdom-minded pastor who understood the high value of prayer once told a 13-year-old boy to never miss a prayer meeting because he never would know when the Spirit might fall. That young man, Evan Roberts, prayed for up to five nights a week for 13 years. Then in 1904, God erupted in love on the sacrificial prayers of Roberts.[9]

BENEFITS OF CORPORATE PRAYER MEETINGS

- They create the atmosphere for God to move.
- They create faith in your church.
- They create a habitation for His presence.
- They create Kingdom encounters.
- They create the platform for people to be easily saved.

|| 21 ||

WEEPING BETWEEN THE PORCH AND THE ALTAR

I don't want to play with marbles…
when God told me to move mountains!
—REINHARD BONNKE

Vesta Mangun, a 96-year-old preacher of the gospel, has seen this world change and shift. She has seen moves of God come and go. She made this observation about revival: "Great revival always begins in the hearts of a few men and women upon whose hearts God lays a burden from which no rest can be found except in desperate crying unto God for an endowment of power from on high that comes through prayer, more prayer, better prayer, fasting prayer, and sleepless prayer."

Her statement could not be more true and fitting for the hour in which we live. Our approach to prayer has to be more than asking for things from a wish list. The posture of our heart has to change.

The question was asked of a person who was present during the Azusa Street Revival, which began in 1906, "In your judgment what was the outstanding spiritual phenomenon of the Azusa Revival?"

The reply: "Without question, in my own judgment, from the spiritual standpoint it can be answered in one word, tears." He said, "I have been a Christian since boyhood and my observation has been that hardness of heart is probably the greatest single obstacle and hindrance to revival." He continued, "The Azusa Street revival began where every revival should begin, in repentant tears. The revival began in tears, it lived in tears, and when the tears ended the Azusa Street revival ended."

This same sentiment is found in the book of Joel when the people of Israel were in desperate need of God's intervention. The hour was beyond critical as the Israelites were on the verge of God's judgment; all knew intense suffering was on the horizon. Even though judgment was justified, God had another plan. God instructed the prophet to relay specific instructions to the priests, "Don't say anything, pray!" God fine-tuned His wishes:

> *Between the temple porch and the altar, let the priests, ministers of the Lord, weep and say, "Have pity upon Your people, and do not make Your heritage a disgrace, a mockery among the nations. Why*

should they say among the peoples, 'Where is their God?'" (Joel 2:17 MEV)

God's instructions in the text above require a closer look. The ancient temple reveals there were three distinct areas— the porch, the altar, and the space in between.

THE PORCH

The porch was located at the front of the sanctuary, and from this purposed position people were allowed to gather together in order to witness the intense scenes unfolding at the altar. In the porch area, the people could clearly see and hear the priests weeping with great intercession for the people they loved. Also, they could look past the interceding priests to a more secluded area—the altar.

THE ALTAR

The altar within the temple was the area where the sacrificial offerings ascended to the Lord. Both death and fire reigned in the altar space. Again, people who were at the temple porch could witness all the activities at the altar. You can only imagine all they heard as the animals that were preparing to be sacrificed squealed in pain and fear. Then, the people saw the enormous amount blood on the altar and on the ground. This area of the temple was messy and unpleasant. Then there was the smell—the horrific, nonstop stench of burning flesh. It's an aroma that one never forgets.

The Space In Between

This an interesting section of the temple. It became a place of intercession and agony of soul for the priests—an area of travail and anguish. The priests were told by God to strategically position themselves between the people and the altar, the place of death. In this special place, the space in the middle, God instructed His priests to assemble in order to weep and wail for the people. No doubt the observers on the porch could see the priests and hear their prayers as they cried out for God to forgo His judgment and to spare His people. They listened closely. The priests prayed that their fellow brethren would turn from their sins to serve the true and only God.

It is because of this place, the space in between, and what happened there that God withdrew His wrath and took another look at His people.

Our Example

We have to get to this place, the *in between place*, literally the place between the living and the dead. We have to be a modern-day Aaron who acquired fire from the altar of the Lord in order to stop a plague from spreading and destroying lives. He did as he was instructed by Moses, *"And he stood between the dead and the living; so the plague was stopped"* (Numbers 16:48 NKJV). Intercession averts danger and can change the trajectory of a person's life as well as a community.

This mandate must not and cannot be treated lightly or ignored. The call to gather together in the middle applies to all of us and not to pastors only. The New Testament declares we are all priests now (see 1 Peter 2:9), and God is calling us to stand in the in-between place in order to aggressively pray, weep, and intercede for those who need His grace and mercy. If we fail to do this, darkness will continue to advance and people will launch themselves into a Christless eternity. Their plight must move us to action.

I heard the story about Hugh Price Hughes, who at one time was a leading voice in the Methodist Church in England. It was said, "When he came back on a Sunday night from the service, if no one had been saved, he would be inconsolable. You couldn't comfort him. He wouldn't eat, he wouldn't drink. He wouldn't even take his long coat off. He threw himself over his bed and he sobbed and he sobbed and he sobbed and said, 'Why? Why? Why?'"[1]

What an example Mr. Hughes demonstrated for us all. One has to ponder how many pastors, evangelists, or leaders live with that level of compassion and concern for the souls of people. How many of us actually go home and cry because no one got saved in our services? When was the last time we wept because the prodigals refused to budge?

> When was the last time we wept because the prodigals refused to budge?

Let's dare to do what Mr. Hughes did. If no one gets saved in the church service you attend, go home, throw yourself across the bed, and weep before God. This may seem extreme, but it moves heaven.

Tears Move God

When Nehemiah heard that his beloved city was destroyed and facing devastating calamity, the Bible says he sat down and cried and mourned for many days (see Nehemiah 1:4).

King David, the man after God's own heart and the greatest king Israel ever had, once said, *"My tears have been my food day and night"* (Psalm 42:3 NKJV). He added in Psalm 126:5-6 (NKJV):

> *Those who sow in tears shall reap in joy. He who continually goes forth weeping, bearing seed for sowing, shall doubtless come again with rejoicing, bringing his sheaves with him.*

And, "All night I make my bed swim; I drench my couch with my tears" (Psalm 6:6 NKJV).

God told the prophet Isaiah in 2 Kings 20:5 (NKJV), *"Return and tell Hezekiah the leader of My people, 'Thus says the Lord, the God of David your father: "I have heard your prayer, I have seen your tears; surely I will heal you."'"*

> *Their heart cried out to the Lord, "O wall of the daughter of Zion, let tears run down like a river day and night; give yourself no relief; give your eyes*

no rest. Arise, cry out in the night, at the beginning of the watches; pour out your heart like water before the face of the Lord. Lift your hands toward Him for the life of your young children, who faint from hunger at the head of every street" (Lamentations 2:18-19 NKJV).

A Jewish scholar says, "The prophet, by the very nature of his calling, is a tragic figure. He has a fierce loyalty toward God and he has a broken heart over a lost and spiritually broken nation."

JESUS WEPT

By God's design, Jerusalem was made the capital of His people during the reign of King David. It was a splendid place and held a special spot in every Jew's heart, especially Jesus'. In Luke 19, Jesus was preparing Himself to enter the city for the last time. His crucifixion was just days away. He purposely stopped and paused on a gently sloping hill that gave Him a panoramic view of the entire city. The view was breathtaking. On this occasion when He looked over the great city of God, He didn't see the majestic walls, cobblestone streets, and beautiful stone structures. No, He saw the terrible fate of the people He loved. He knew due to their rejection of Him, suffering and pain were in their future. This moved Him to tears. The text says He wept.

Now as He drew near, He saw the city and wept over it, saying, "If you had known, even you, especially in this your day, the things that make for your peace! But now they are hidden from your eyes" (Luke 19:41-42 NKJV).

Jesus cried! The Greek word for *wept* in verse 41 is *klaio*, and it means "weeping as a sign of pain and grief; to mourn as if crying over the dead; to wail out loud."[2] Can you see the event unfolding now? Jesus approaches the city and becomes overwhelmed with emotion; He begins to audibly weep as if He has just heard the news that someone precious to Him has died. This isn't a single tear scrolling down His cheek and then He moves on. No, He is gripped by the moment and the harsh reality that His people rejected Him and His free offer of deliverance and salvation. He feels the full weight of that rejection and its forthcoming consequences.

This is how Jesus responded to His culture; He set the example for us. The question must be asked—how long has it been since we wept before the Lord over the spiritual condition of our children and friends? Furthermore, when was the last time we lost sleep and cried out to God for our church due to no revival? Can we recall when we've wept for our pastors and the leaders of the church?

Someone has to run to the in-between place and weep and pray! And history has revealed a harsh truth: a church that will not, cannot, and has not shed tears will never have revival.

|| 22 ||

FILL THE BOWL

*We must begin to believe that God, in the
mystery of prayer, has entrusted us with a
force that can move the Heavenly world,
and can bring its power down to earth.*
—ANDREW MURRAY

I am convinced the devil doesn't fear us—he fears the God
of Abraham, Isaac, and Jacob. However, his eyes are ever
toward the praying ones. I am persuaded the devil has a
strong hatred for those who pray. He loathes the praying
soul. Why? Satan fears what can happen when through our
prayers we bring the full might, strength, and power of the
Kingdom of heaven to the earth. The devil knows if and when
a believer truly lays hold of God through prayer, the foundations of the kingdom of darkness are disrupted. When we
pray, not only do our prayers commission angels on divine

assignments, our prayers also release Kingdom realities upon the earth.

There are two significant passages in the book of Revelation that need our attention:

> *And when he had taken it, the four living creatures and the twenty-four elders fell down before the Lamb. Each one had a harp and they were holding golden bowls full of incense, which are the prayers of God's people* (Revelation 5:8 NIV).
>
> *When he opened the seventh seal, there was silence in heaven for about half an hour. And I saw the seven angels who stand before God, and seven trumpets were given to them. Another angel, who had a golden censer, came and stood at the altar. He was given much incense to offer, with the prayers of all God's people, on the golden altar in front of the throne. The smoke of the incense, together with the prayers of God's people, went up before God from the angel's hand. Then the angel took the censer, filled it with fire from the altar, and hurled it on the earth; and there came peals of thunder, rumblings, flashes of lightning and an earthquake* (Revelation 8:1-5 NIV).

In this passage, the Lord allows us to see the activity deep in the throne room of God. The seventh seal is opened. This seventh seal is the last page of history. And throughout the area there is silence—nothing is being said. Seven heavenly angels stand before God and are given seven trumpets. Then another angel appears and approaches the altar carrying a bowl (or censer) of incense to present to God the prayers of the saints.

Think of this—the prayers of the saints are delivered before the throne of God. The imagery is fascinating. The angel takes the prayer bowl, which is filled with your prayers, to the altar of fire and then the angel rakes the flames into the bowl. Then, holding this bowl of fire mixed with our prayers, he steps over the ledge and hurls it onto the earth. The result? The earth shook: *"thunder, rumblings, flashes of lightning and an earthquake"* (Revelation 8:5 NIV).

Let this ignite your heart to pray more. Look, none of your faith-filled prayers are wasted. They are not meaningless—they are before the Lord. Fill the bowl! Keep asking. Keep petitioning the Lord. The task at hand demands us to pray with greater focus and fervency. The desires in your heart are huge and the opposition to them is real. Our adversary is legitimate and strong; however, your persistence is greater. Don't let up—keep praying.

> **The desires in your heart are huge and the opposition to them is real. Our adversary is legitimate and strong; however, your persistence is greater.**

Let me explain this a little more. It is important to see that every situation you take to prayer has its individual bowl. For example, your finances have a bowl, your children have a bowl, your career has a bowl, the friend who has stage 4 cancer has a bowl. Furthermore, I believe there are different-sized bowls considering the seriousness of the issue. Praying for the Lord to get you into the college of your choice isn't the same as praying for your prodigal son who has a twelve-year addiction to meth. They are each important to you but not equal. One has little spiritual resistance, while the other has multiple layers of flesh, soul ties, and demonic activity swirling about. The size of the bowl in order to release the will of God is different as well. Therefore, it is possible it will take longer to get the answer you desire concerning the prodigal. The prodigal's "prayer bowl" is larger because you are dealing with more than getting an application approved by a college. We have to see that each case requires a different strategy, and because the prayer bowl for the prodigal is much larger, you don't give up—you keep praying until the bowl is full.

Keep praying until the bowl is full.

How do you know the bowl is full? There is a note of peace and victory that comes to your soul. It is unexplainable. You feel a shift and God says, "It is done!" You persevered and kept filling the bowl, you didn't give up when you saw no improvement, but you remained faithful to pray. Therefore, the battle has been won—the forces of evil have been defeated. When this happens, you transition from petitioning the Lord to a posture of praise and thanksgiving.

We must change our mindset that believes one prayer is always enough. It may be in some situations, but in most cases it is not—we must faithfully pray until the bowl is full. Praying that makes a difference is hard work. It is labor-intensive and demands perseverance. Galatians 6:9 promises we will see the answer if we do not give up. Jesus taught His disciples, *"men always ought to pray and not lose heart"* (Luke 18:1 NKJV).

Mary Warburton Booth understood this value when she said, "I do not think he [the devil] minds our praying about things if we leave it at that. What he minds, and opposes steadily, is the prayer that prays on until it is prayed through, assured of the answer."[1]

My dear friend, don't grow weary—God is hearing, listening, and accumulating your prayers. When you pray in faith, none of your prayers will ever be ignored, forgotten, misplaced, or considered ineffectual. They are accumulating before the throne of God. Keep asking, keep seeking, keep knocking until the bowl overflows!

The Power of Persistence

No one in American history exemplifies persistence more than the 16th president of the United States, Abraham Lincoln. He had every reason to remain average, to withdraw from public life, but he didn't. Here are a few things he overcame—he failed in business at the age of 21. He was soundly defeated in a legislative race one year later at the age of 22. He failed again at business at age 24, then overcame the tragic death of his lover at age 26. Then, when he was at the young age of 27, he suffered a nervous breakdown. And once again, he lost a congressional race at 34 and 36, lost a senatorial race at 45, failed to become vice president at 47, lost a senatorial race at 49, and then finally was elected president of the United States of America at age 52.

Think for a minute what direction this nation would have taken if he had not decided to keep pushing forward through all of his setbacks and failures.

One of the greatest restaurant chains in America is Kentucky Fried Chicken. It really is "finger-lickin' good." People look at the iconic image of the restaurant and may assume the founder, Colonel Sanders, has always been in the restaurant business. However, what you may not know is that Colonel Sanders was a military retiree and was living on a small pension with little to nothing to his name; he found himself penniless. In fact, his first social security check was for one hundred and five dollars. However, there is one thing he possessed—his mother's recipe for fried chicken. He set out to sell his mom's chicken recipe to restaurants and was rejected 1,007 times before someone bought it. That one "yes" changed his life and Kentucky Fried Chicken was birthed.

Perseverance doesn't come naturally; it is a choice of the will. Everything on the inside of you resists it. In fact, you have to force yourself to take another step, to get up and try again.

What is the typical response when we don't get an immediate answer to our prayers? Often, we are prone to stop praying. However, this is not what the Bible teaches us we should do. In fact, we should do the exact opposite—not stop praying, but pray more. Keep asking, keep knocking, and keep seeking.

The Lord understood the value and necessity of persistence when it comes to prayer. He knew we would face discouragement when we don't receive immediate answers from our prayers. The word *persistent* means "relentless, continual, constant, and tenacious." In essence, to persevere means to never give up! Does this describe your posture during prayer? If not, adjust your demeanor and keep at it until you fill the bowl. I love what Martin Luther said, "Prayer is not overcoming God's reluctance, but laying hold of His willingness." The Lord is willing—keep praying!

This truth is echoed in Jesus' teaching in Luke 11:9-10 (NKJV):

> *So I say to you, ask, and it will be given to you; seek, and you will find; knock, and it will be opened to you. For everyone who asks receives, and he who seeks finds, and to him who knocks it will be opened.*

The three words Jesus used—*ask, seek, knock*—are in the present tense imperative mood in the Greek language, which suggests that the person praying needs to "keep on asking until they receive, keep on seeking until they find, and keep on knocking until the door is opened." Unequivocally, with this teaching Jesus is inviting each of us to pray and not to relent until the answer comes.

Along this same theme, Jesus shared an unusual parable in Luke 18. The subject matter was the necessity of persistence when it comes to prayer.

> *Then He spoke a parable to them, that men always ought to pray and not lose heart, saying: "There was in a certain city a judge who did not fear God nor regard man. Now there was a widow in that city; and she came to him, saying, 'Get justice for me from my adversary.' And he would not for a while; but afterward he said within himself, 'Though I do not fear God nor regard man, yet because this widow troubles me I will avenge her, lest by her continual coming she weary me.'"*
>
> *Then the Lord said, "Hear what the unjust judge said. And shall God not avenge His own elect who cry out day and night to Him, though He bears long with them? I tell you that He will avenge them speedily. Nevertheless, when the Son of Man comes, will He really find faith on the earth?"* (Luke 18:1-8 NKJV)

The Lord began the text with a sobering reminder. In verse 1, He said that we are to pray always and to not lose heart. It was setting the tone that effective prayer takes time and perseverance.

In the parable, the Lord pitted a poor, powerless person (the widow) against a powerful and influential judge. What did she desire? Justice. The situation the widow was facing is unknown to us; perhaps it had to do with the untimely death of her husband, and she was seeking the judge to bring justice to the situation. Whatever the issue was, she felt justified in asking the judge for justice to be served. She was adamant about what she knew; the case was clear to her. The text reveals that she would not let the judge forget her case. She was relentless in her appeal to him.

In verse 4, the judge would not release a verdict on her case. The text reveals he knew about the case for some time. However, it got to the point that he was so relentlessly agitated by her he said, *"yet because this widow troubles me I will avenge her"* (Luke 18:5 NKJV).

Let's break this verse down. First, the Greek word for *trouble* is *parechō,* which means "to present evidence, to show, and even to trouble someone."[2] Then he said he would "avenge" her, which means "I will respond and make this thing right. I will protect her, defend her, and punish the person who did the injustice."[3] Wow! This is remarkable. Why did he all of a sudden decide to render a verdict on the case? Well, he revealed why at the end of verse 5, *"lest by her continual coming she weary me."*

There are two important words that reveal to us why he responded—*continual* and *weary*. The Greek word for *continual* is *telos*, which means "one who endures to the end."[4] This implies she didn't stop until she got what she knew was right. She persevered until the answer came.

Next, the Greek word for *weary* is *hypōpiazō*, and it means to "beat black and blue, to smite so as to cause bruises." In addition it means "to give one intolerable annoyance, to wear one out."[5]

Don't miss why Jesus was sharing this parable. He directly connected it to prayer. He was strongly implying this is how we should pray; this is how we should approach Him. This text does not imply that we should be irreverent or arrogant, shaking our fists, demanding He do something. No, His emphasis is on the persistence of prayer. We should always approach the Lord with humility, brokenness, and reverence, persistent in knowing the Father's goodwill toward us and His desire to answer us. In Jesus' explanation of the parable, He made the point that if persistence worked in this widow's dire situation, how much more will it work with a loving and just God!

A persistent spirit is the foundation for releasing the will of God in your life and on the earth.

THEY KEEP ASKING FOR ICE CREAM

I said it earlier, but it bears repeating—a persistent spirit is the foundation for releasing the will of God in your life and on the earth. Asking the Lord more than once is not an indication of a lack of faith, but actually in most cases, it is a demonstration of your faith. For example, when you are out with your family and your child asks you for an ice cream cone, they truly believe they will receive. When you ignore their request or act like you didn't hear them or respond with a "No, not now," it doesn't stop them; it doesn't even seem to faze them. What do they typically do? They ask again. Then when you say, "No, I am not buying you an ice cream cone, don't ask again," what do they do? They ask again, and this time with a more desperate and emphatic tone. Here is the truth—they don't ask you again thinking they won't receive; they ask knowing they will receive if they keep asking. Their goal is to wear you down and break your reluctance to give them what they desire—ice cream. And when they weary you with their redundancy, you give in and buy them an ice cream cone.

Jesus spoke this parable to insure us that your persistency matters and it is perfectly fine to approach Him frequently and with a fervent spirit. The phrase in verse 7 says God will avenge those who *"cry out day and night to Him, though He bears long with them."* This is an indication that God expects you to frequently pray about the same thing over and over. Again, as the text reveals, the answer may not come quickly, but according to verse 8 when you fill the bowl the answer will come speedily.

Keep asking for ice cream!

23

FIVE LANES OF PRAYER

(DR. KAREN SMITH)

*Prayer will be the primary anointing of the
end-time church. Fueled by the Holy Spirit and the knowledge of her bridal identity,*
—COREY RUSSELL, *Prayer: Why
Our Words to God Matter*

Freeways across America offer multiple lanes in which vehi-
cles can travel. Generally there is an entrance lane, a couple
of middle lanes, and finally the *fast lane!* All cars on the freeway move in the same direction. A driver may move from
one lane to another as the need arises, enabling them to
pass another car, increase their speed, or get into a comfort-
able spot to go the distance. Each lane offers different speed
expectations, and a driver chooses what lane will best accom-
modate them in order to successfully reach their destination.

In many ways, prayer is like a freeway. When we enter into a time of prayer, we are all going in the same direction with a destination in mind—seeing our prayers answered to the glory of God. Sometimes we move fast in prayer due to a sense of urgency, and other times we move slow, taking our time and enjoying fellowship with the Lord. And as with a freeway, there are multiple lanes of prayer in which we can travel. Maybe you never thought of prayer in this way, but it is a great analogy. There are various lanes or types of prayer. Each lane serves a particular purpose in getting us to our destination—answered prayer!

Choose Your Lane

What prayer lane we choose to travel in depends on the type of need or situation we bring before the Lord. Let's take a look at the different types of prayer as seen in the Bible, all of which serve a particular purpose at a particular time in a believer's life.

Philippians 4:6-7 (KJV) lets us in on at least four *types* of prayer.

> *Be careful for nothing; but in every thing by prayer and supplication with thanksgiving let your requests be made known unto God. And the peace of God, which passeth all understanding, shall keep your hearts and minds through Christ Jesus.*

The fifth lane is *intercession* and will also be covered here.

Lane #1

The first lane of prayer in this passage is *prayer* itself! Prayer (*proseuche*[1]), in and of itself, is a prayer lane and would be considered the slow lane or even a frontage road. We travel in this prayer lane when we simply want to talk to God and meet with Him on a regular basis. It's the word used most often for Jesus' prayers. It suggests an intimacy with God. There are no Thees and Thous, but rather heart-to-heart and face-to-face requests and conversation. This is the type of prayer we pray all day and every day. In this lane, we approach God as our Friend.

Lane #2

The next type of prayer or prayer lane we see in this passage is *supplication*. We might consider this a fast lane of prayer. The original word for *supplication* is the Greek word *deesis*. By definition, it indicates a need or a lack in one's life.[2] When a person comes to God in supplication, they will plead strongly with God for a need to be met or an area of lack to be filled. This word comes from a root word that literally means "to beg." A person praying in this lane needs God's immediate provision and attention.

An example of supplication (*deesis*) is found in James 5:16 (NKJV):

> *Confess your trespasses to one another, and pray for one another, that you may be healed. The effective, fervent prayer [deesis] of a righteous man avails much.*

This type of prayer is intentional, focused, determined, serious, and earnest. When we have a deep need in our lives, we should not be shy in bringing it to the Lord and earnestly contending for the need to be met.

> **When we have a deep need in our lives, we should not be shy in bringing it to the Lord and earnestly contending for the need to be met.**

The idea of *begging* as mentioned above should not be interpreted as God sitting in heaven with His arms crossed, daring us to come to Him with a need, and if we *beg* long enough and hard enough He will answer. James 1:5 indicates when we ask God for something, He grants a gift *liberally and without reproach*. In his expanded translation of the New Testament, Kenneth S. Wuest translates the verse this way:

> *Let him keep on presenting his request in the presence of the giving God who gives to all with simplicity and without reserve [a pure, simple giving of good without admixture of evil or bitterness], and who does not [with the giving of the gift] reproach [the recipient with any manifestation of displeasure or regret], and it shall be given him.*

Keep in mind the most important attribute of God—He is *good*. He is not startled by our cry when we are in need. It gives Him great pleasure to meet our need according to His riches in glory!

Lane #3

Another lane of prayer mentioned in Philippians 4:6 is *thanksgiving* or *adoration*. This type of prayer does not have a need, a desire, or a want attached to it. We pray in the lane of thanksgiving when we simply recall the wondrous works and ways of the Lord. We give thanks to the Lord when we praise Him for what He has done with a heart of gratitude. The word for *thanksgiving* here is a compound of the words *eu* and *charis*. *Eu* basically means *good* and *charis* is the Greek word for grace. These two words together form the word *eucharistos* (*thanksgiving*) which describes an outpouring of grace and wonder that freely flows from one's heart in response to the acts of God. The idea is that your heart is so swollen with gratitude over the goodness of God that you cannot help but thank Him over and over again. Your heart beams with appreciation for all He has done for you, and you exalt Him continuously, unashamedly, and out loud![3] Imagine spending time simply reflecting on all God has done and genuinely *thanking Him for His goodness and faithfulness!*

Unfortunately, thanksgiving is probably the prayer lane least traveled. So many times we come to God in prayer because we have a dream, a desire, a complaint, a problem, or a situation that needs His immediate attention. What if we spent time in prayer reminding God of all He has done since the beginning of time? As we meditate on His creation, His blessings, His provision, His miracles, and His wonders, we begin to adore Him and thank Him for all His mighty deeds! Just as parents desire gratitude and thankfulness from their children, God desires His children come to Him in thanksgiving and *"bless His holy name"* (Psalm 103:1 NKJV).

Here is something else to consider regarding thanksgiving. It is a great expression of faith when we give thanks to God in prayer *before* the answer to our prayer comes about. Thanksgiving displays a level of trust and confidence in the God who is faithful to hear and answer prayer. And the passion and intensity of our thanksgiving should match the passion and intensity of our prayers!

> **Thanksgiving displays a level of trust and confidence in the God who is faithful to hear and answer prayer.**

Lane #4

The fourth prayer lane mentioned in the Philippians passage is *requests*. In his book *Sparkling Gems from the Greek*, Rick Renner gives a powerful expanded definition of this type of prayer. The Greek word *aitima* (requests) is used in this passage and it comes from the root word *aiteo*. *Aiteo* means, "to be adamant in requesting and demanding assistance to meet tangible needs, such as food, shelter, money, and so forth." In the New Testament, this word is used to describe "a person who insists or demands that a specific need be met after approaching and speaking to his superior with respect and honor." Look again at that statement, "...after approaching and speaking to his superior with respect and honor." Often in our urgency to have our needs met, we are quick to bring Him our requests before we take the time to honor and reverence Him. Imagine how a parent feels when their child comes to them with a request or desire without first expressing appreciation or gratitude for the blessings they have already received. It is important to take time to express our love for the Lord and our gratitude to Him for His faithfulness and goodness to us *before* we bring Him our needs. He appreciates and responds to honor and He is certainly worthy of it!

As one prays in this manner, there is full expectation that what is being requested will be granted without hesitation.

When we come to God in this prayer lane, we can stand confident in His goodness and faithfulness to meet our needs. His response to us is based on *His goodness* as our Father and His willingness to provide for us. It is never based on our own merit. We come to the Lord fully convinced that He is good and He is more than willing to take care of our needs.

Psalm 66:17-20 (ESV) says:

> *I cried to him with my mouth, and high praise was on my tongue. If I had cherished iniquity in my heart, the Lord would not have listened. But truly God has listened; he has attended to the voice of my*

prayer. Blessed be God, because he has not rejected my prayer or removed his steadfast love from me!

It is because of His *steadfast love* for us that we can come boldly before Him and make our *requests* before Him and, yes, even be adamant about it! Keep in mind the above definition. We must always approach the Lord with the utmost respect, honor, and gratitude when we appeal to Him in prayer.

Lane #5

The fifth type of prayer is what I consider to be the *fast lane of prayer* and that is *intercession*. This form of prayer shows up in both the Old and New Testaments. When speaking prophetically of the coming Messiah, the prophet Isaiah said, "*He bore the sin of many, and made* intercession *for the transgressors*" (Isaiah 53:12 NKJV). In chapter 27, Jeremiah instructed the true prophets of the Lord to *intercede* with the Lord regarding the vessels of the temple, entreating Him to protect the vessels from being violated or stolen by the Babylonians.

In the New Testament, the word *intercession* appears in several passages. In Romans 8:26, the Bible says the Holy Spirit *makes intercession for us*. Hebrews 7:25 says Jesus makes intercession for the saints. In 1 Timothy 2:1, Paul instructed Timothy to *make intercession* for all men.

When we hear the word *intercession* in the church community, we have a general idea of what it means, or at least what we think it means for us. Most would define inter-cession as an aggressive, gut-wrenching, emotional form of prayer. It is generally understood as urgent prayer for a press-ing matter or for a person in desperate need. All of these ideas are true, but where does the sense of urgency and pas-sion come from that causes one to position themselves in the prayer lane of intercession from time to time?

> **Where does the sense of urgency and passion come from that causes one to position themselves in the prayer lane of intercession from time to time?**

The answer is realized when we understand the mean-ing of the words used in the scripture for *intercession*. The Hebrew word for *intercession* is *paga*, which means "to strike or light upon by chance."[5] One Greek word for *intercession* is *huperentugchano*, which means "to fall in with or to chance upon."[6] These meanings indicate an almost sudden or unex-pected encounter or an intersection of sorts. Think about it. Have you ever been minding your own business, going about your day, and all of a sudden someone comes to your mind whom you weren't even thinking about (intersection!) and you sense a strong call to hit your knees and pray for them? All of a sudden you find yourself interceding for them with intensity and focus. You sense urgency, as if time is of the essence, and you do whatever you must to drive hard in the prayer lane of intercession.

Intercession is also defined as "pleading with one on behalf of another." And isn't that what happens when we sense a pulling to pray for someone the Lord has brought to mind? We go before the throne on behalf of someone and plead before the Father for them in intercession. A spirit of intercession can come upon us from the Lord for people, nations, governments, in the event of a sudden accident, a life-threatening situation, wars, or in a time of testing.

When we intercede, we "fall in" with the person and stand alongside them in prayer, pleading on their behalf for divine intervention from heaven. We pray for what the individual needs. We pray in tongues (in the Spirit) when we don't know exactly how to pray for an individual (see Romans 8:26). We declare and decree and the heavenly realm responds. Subsequently, we are minimizing opposition and activating the fullness of God's resources to be released in order to fulfill God's desire in the person's life.

We should be ever aware, ever conscious of those times of *divine intersection* when a God-thought crosses our path and instantly we are interrupted with an urgent call to prayer. We must refrain from thinking that it is merely happenstance that a person's face or name flashes across our mind. No, it's *not happenstance*. It very well could be the Lord engaging you in intercession for someone!

For example, let's say you are driving to work one morning, minding your own business, when all of a sudden the image of your mom's friend comes to mind. You say to yourself, *That's weird. Why in the world am I thinking about her?* And immediately you push the thought away and continue driving, never giving the image a second thought.

What if the image was from the Lord? What if the Lord is prompting you to intercede for this friend because she is in trouble, maybe in another state or city, and she needs help? The Lord responds to the prayers of His people and He needs you to pray! But you don't realize it is a prompting from Him to intercede and you pay no attention to what is brought to mind. The friend has no prayer protection if you don't realize what is happening when their face comes to your mind "out of nowhere." It is not a coincidence. It is the Lord calling you to pray on behalf of the friend. It is *paga,* "a divine intersection" between you and the Lord—your thoughts are interrupted by an image He sends. It is time to intercede.

There are many more prayer lanes exhibited in the Bible such as warfare, confession, lament, and petitioning. There is even a prayer lane called *burach,* a common practice among the Jews, when in prayer one asks for nothing from the Lord, but simply speaks to *bless the Lord.* Almost every Jewish prayer starts with the words *burach ata Adonai*—"Blessed are You, our Lord." This is a practice Christians would do well to embrace more often.

Burach is more than thanksgiving. The focus is on the majesty and greatness of God! It is the difference between, let's say, thanking God for the food we eat and thanking

God that He is *the only One* who can make food come out of the ground! See the difference? Rather than thanking Him for what He provides, we thank Him that He has the might and the power to *make and create* what He provides!

Another example is, in thanking God for creation, one would pray, "Blessed is He who did not omit anything from the world and created within it good creations and good trees for people to enjoy!" In times of storm, rather than asking God to remove it, one would pray, "Blessed is He whose strength and power fill the world!" When one goes through a hard time, rather than asking God, "Why?" or complaining, we pray, "Blessed is He who is the true judge." In other words, God is good and deals justly with mankind for our good. This is a prayer lane Western Christians would do well to embrace more often.

Not every prayer encounter with the Lord is the same. The cry of your heart and the need of the hour will often determine the lane in which you pray. Sometimes we need to determine *what lane is open*, what type of prayer effort is needed in the moment. Do we need to engage in intercession and power through for someone? Is there a call for thanksgiving when the request has been made and we need only to *thank Him* for the answer? What if all other lanes are closed and there is a desperate need for supplication in the spirit where we bring a *request* to God with a great expectation of seeing a need met?

Verbal Bean (1933–1977) was a gifted man of God who possessed great insights. One of his ideas involved these types of prayer, what he called "channels of the Spirit." He taught that when we pray, we should be sensitive to which channel or lane of the Spirit is open. At certain times or seasons, God opens only one lane. We may spend much time with supplication when what He desires from us is thanksgiving. Or, we desire simply to talk with the Lord when He needs us to stand in the gap and intervene for someone else.

Whatever the need or the concern, there is an avenue, a lane of prayer, we can move into to meet the final destination—to see the Lord glorified as He answers the prayers of His children.

24

HOW TO PRAY FOR THE UNSAVED

Men may spurn our appeals, reject our message, oppose our arguments, despise our persons, but they are helpless against our prayers.
—J. SIDLOW BAXTER

According to the Bible, every person will spend eternity in one of two places—heaven or hell. In his book *Caught Up Into Paradise,* Dr. Richard Eby gives a few details of his two-minute vision of hell. He said, "Instantly I realized I was a dead sinner being taken to the lowest bowels of the earth. A sense of absolute terror gripped my being." In this pit, small spider-like demons were crawling all over him in total darkness and isolation. He said he knew he would never see another person; he would never get out. Demons would taunt him:

"Damn God! Damn people!" And the smell! Horrid, nasty, stale, fetid, rotten and evil... mixed together and concentrated. Stinking, crawling demons mentally delighting in making me wretched. My terror mounted until I was ready to collapse into utter hopelessness, crushing despair, abysmal loneliness. I was an eternally lost soul by my own choosing...The clammy wet walls held me crushed for eternity without escape.[1]

The above description of hell is horrific, and none of us want the people we love to spend eternity in such a terrible place. Below is how you can pray for those who are unsaved in order for them to become born again.

Let us begin with letting the richness of James 5:16 seep into our hearts. This verse gives all the assurance that our prayers matter and can make a difference.

> *The heartfelt and persistent prayer of a righteous man (believer) can accomplish much [when put into action and made effective by God—it is dynamic and can have tremendous power]* (James 5:16 AMP).

For starters, realize your prayers have dynamic power against the enemy. He knows this and hates it when you pray, especially when you pray for those you love to leave his family.

> **Your prayers have dynamic power against the enemy.**

It is important to note, when you are praying for some-one to be saved, the darkness upon their life is great and the enemy is deeply entrenched. Perhaps they have opened unthinkable doors to sin and evil over their lives. As with every situation, it will take much prayer to weaken the ene-my's position. It may take some time before they fall under conviction and are converted. Often, when we don't see an immediate reaction to our prayers, we give up or quit, so the word of the Lord to you is, "Don't quit. Don't stop because you are not seeing results." If you quit, the net result will be that the devil will reinforce the territory you were able to gain through your prayers. Keep praying!

Think about the value of what you are doing. When you pray for someone, you are standing in a significant gap. What gap? You stand in the middle, centered between the will of God for someone's life and the evil the devil intends for them. You are interceding for God's will to be done over them, and you are opposing the agenda of the devil. I cannot stress how important this is, and it must not be taken lightly. When we pray for the unsaved, we are actually preparing the way for the Holy Spirit to gain uninhibited access to their minds and hearts so they can be receptive to the conviction and pull of the Holy Spirit.

Have you ever wondered how an unsaved person can hear a beautiful and clear presentation of the gospel and yet be unmoved? Second Corinthians 4:3-4 (NKJV) reveals why the unsaved resist the gospel and what we can do about it.

But even if our gospel is veiled, it is veiled to those who are perishing, whose minds the god of this age has blinded, who do not believe, lest the light of the gospel of the glory of Christ, who is the image of God, should shine on them.

BREAKING IT DOWN

This text gives us hope. It reveals satan's plan for the unsaved and how we can counter his agenda and bring conversion to the ones we love. First, let's take a close look at a key phrase within the verse: *"whose minds the god of this age has blinded."*

Satan plays an active role in keeping our friends away from God. He does this by blinding their minds. The god of this world, satan, seeks to keep people blinded to the truth. Even though the message of Jesus is simple, the average unsaved person doesn't see the validity and value of it. Certainly, they think it is good, sweet, and necessary for some, but not just them. I have witnessed this thousands of times throughout the years. So the devil's primary role it to keep them in darkness, unconcerned about their spiritual plight or standing before God. Because satan has placed layers of darkness over them, it is difficult for the light of the gospel, the truth of the good news, to penetrate to their heart.

You Don't Have to Ask God to Save Them

Because I know the devil's activity and intent in keeping people unsaved, I do not have to spend my time trying to talk God into saving them. Why? There is no reason for me to try to convince the Lord into saving them because I already know He is willing to save them. You and I both have been to prayer meetings, and it seems our prayers are begging God to save our friends. For example, we pray, "Lord, will You save Tony? God, he really needs You, so please save him?" The person who prays this has a pure heart, but honestly this prayer is a waste of time. Why? God has already proven He wants to save everyone, including "Tony."

The Lord is not slack concerning His promise, as some count slackness, but is longsuffering toward us, not willing that any should perish but that all should come to repentance (2 Peter 3:9 NKJV).

In this situation, God is not the problem. He is not the obstacle—satan is. God is already willing to save Tony; God is waiting on him to respond favorably to the pull of the Holy Spirit. However, Tony cannot feel the pull of the Holy Spirit due to his eyes being blind to the truth.

God is not the problem. He is not the obstacle—satan is.

I believe if Tony heard the good news without being demonically influenced, he would believe. I must stress this point again—the text reveals the god of this world has blinded his eyes. He is standing in the way of Tony's salvation. The devil will do all he can to keep Tony in his family; he will work around the clock to keep the light of the gospel away from him. Once more, it is satan's blinders on Tony that keep him from being saved. God is not the problem, the devil is the problem!

Radar Jamming

According to the National Transportation Safety Board, in 2019 there were 1,301 plane crashes involving private planes, business jets, and chartered aircraft in the United States.[2]

Whenever air traffic control loses radar contact with an aircraft, it is called "radar contact lost." This means the aircraft's exact position in the air is lost and radar service is no longer being provided. Therefore, the pilot is flying the plane without any assistance, guidance, or protection. In many cases, when radar contact is lost, it results in a crash and loss of life.

During the summer months, our community swimming pool was the place to be. We loved going! Every day all of my friends would go. However, at certain times we had an unwanted guest—the younger sibling of my friend. I remember hearing my neighbor's mom telling my friend, "If you want to go, you have to take your brother." And she would always say, "Keep an eye on him." In others words, don't let anything happen to him, or even worse, don't lose him.

Ironically, I believe the devil communicates this exact message to his demons when it comes to lost people: "Keep an eye on them, watch them closely, and whatever you do don't lose them." Demons work hard and do all within their power to keep unsaved people from coming into contact with the gospel. And if they do hear the gospel, the demons, through various means, will quickly try to devalue it and limit further contact with it.

When radio contact is lost, the individual is on their own. They make decisions based upon what they believe is best for them.

The prayer ministry of a church should be so strong and spiritually violent that when an unsaved person gets within close proximity of that church, the enemy should lose his influence and spiritual leverage with that person. The Spirit of God neutralizes the devil's voice and agenda, and for a brief time the light of the gospel becomes compelling and clear.

My prayer is that every lost person who drives by our church or who ventures onto our property will feel the weightiness of the Holy Spirit's deep conviction and abruptly see their need for Jesus. This type of encounter only happens when we, the Church, reach a certain realm of prayer.

HERE IS HOW I PRAY

First, my prayer should command the devil to cease and desist his activity in Jesus' name. That's right: "Devil, I command you right now to stop your activity and to remove the blinders from Tony's life. Every obstacle, every excuse is cast down now and removed—I command it in Jesus' name." You pray and command this until you know the devil is responding and removing the obstacles. You pray until the devil submits to your demands. There are probably multiple layers of resistance and darkness over Tony's life. Peel them off one layer at a time. This may take some time; be persistent and diligent. Whatever you do, don't give up because you don't see any change in his life. Don't forget, you are in a battle for the soul the devil has legally incarcerated. He doesn't want to let it go; you fight tenaciously for them. If you do not give up, you will prevail and the precious soul will be open to respond to the good news.

> *If you do not give up, you will prevail and the precious soul will be open to respond to the good news.*

Note: I have discovered people usually get worse before the breakthrough comes. Prepare yourself for this and do not let it discourage you. Why do they get worse? The devil knows he is losing ground and tries to tighten things up by attempting to add other layers of darkness over them.

Second, as the blinders are being removed, pray they would fall under terrible conviction as they become aware of their sinfulness and separation from God.

Third, pray that the fear of God would fall upon them and at the same time an awareness of the goodness of God.

Fourth, pray that God's voice would be heard and irresistible as God calls them out of the darkness. I ask the Lord to use dreams, visions, and natural circumstances to speak to their heart.

Fifth, pray for God to strategically maneuver Christ-loving believers into their life who will demonstrate authentic Christianity without hypocrisy.

> *Then He said to His disciples, "The harvest truly is plentiful, but the laborers are few. Therefore pray the Lord of the harvest to send out laborers into His harvest"* (Matthew 9:37-38 NKJV).

If you pray the above consistently and when the Lord moves upon your heart, you will see things change and the grip of the enemy on their life will be broken.

HOW WILL I KNOW VICTORY IS WON?

You will know the battle for their salvation is won when you get a note of victory in your spirit. A peace will come to you that is unexplainable. You will know in your heart that the enemy's plans for your loved one have been defeated. This is a time for thanksgiving and rejoicing. Then, usually in short order, you will see with your own eyes the person you prayed for is becoming more open and receptive to the Lord, and eventually they will repent of their sins and make Jesus their Lord.

Notes

1 Die Well

1. Kathryn Kuhlman, "Knowing the Holy Spirit," Oral Roberts University, Oklahoma, 1972, https://youtu.be/FMMVWN1BBUs?t=1831.
2. T.M. Anderson, *Prayer Availeth Much* (Circleville, OH: The Advocate Publishing House, 1950), https://www.sermonindex.net/modules/bible_books/?view=book_chapter&chapter=47733.
3. Philip E. Howard, Jr., *The Life and Diary of David Brainerd* (Orlando, FL: Creation House), 312.

2 Two Prayers That Changed the World

1. Andrew Dragos, "7 Quick Facts About Billy Graham," March 2, 2018, https://seedbed.com/7-quick-facts-about-billy-graham.
2. Billy Graham Evangelistic Association, "Billy Graham's Father and the Prayer Heard Arond the World," November 4, 2021, https://billygraham.org/story/billy-grahams-father-prayer-heard-around-world.
3. Ibid.
4. "The Prayer Life of Billy Graham," accessed June 7, 2022, https://lightfeatherstoriesw.home.blog/2020/09/18/the-prayer-life-of-billy-graham/amp.

3 The Strong Man Has Been Bound!

1. Taken from a Navigators newsletter, but modified for this context.

4 God Is Limited

1. Myles Munroe, *Understanding the Purpose and Power of Prayer* (New Kensington, PA: Whitaker House, 2018), 19.
2. John Wesley, *A Plain Account of Christian Perfection*, Chapter 11: "Rseflections," 1766.
3. Watchman Nee, *Secrets to Spiritual Power* (New Kensington, PA: Whitaker House, 1999), 88-89.

5 Your Voice Matters

1. Torrey, *The Power of Prayer*, 81.
2. Bishop Samuel Smith, *Profiles in Prayer* (Evansville, IN: 21st Century Reformation Hour), 50.
3. E.M. Bounds, *The Complete Works of E.M. Bounds on Prayer* (Grand Rapids, MI: Baker Books, 2004), 205.

6 Uncommon Power!

1. Andrew Murray, *With Christ in the School of Prayer* (New Kensington, PA: Whitaker House, 1981), 9.
2. "Charles Finney, "Men Who Saw Revival," accessed June 2, 2022, http:// menwhosawrevival.blogspot.com/p/charles-finney.html.
3. Colin Dye, "Smith Wigglesworth on Prayer," March 4, 2013, https:// colindye.com/2013/03/04/smith-wigglesworth-on-prayer.
4. Charlie Shamp, *Mystical Prayer* (Warsaw, IN: Tall Pine Books, 2018), 5.

7 The Mountain Is Sleeping

1. Eric Mack, "Mauna Loa, The World's Biggest Volcano, Is Waking Up and It's Time to Prep for an Eruption," Forbes, March 12, 2021, https://www.forbes.com/sites/ericmack/2021/03/12/mauna-loa-the -worlds-biggest-volcano-is-waking-up-and-its-time-to-prep-for-an -eruption/?sh=74c02ca4d425.
2. US Geological Survey, "How many active volcanoes are there on Earth?" accessed June 3, 2022, https://www.usgs.gov/faqs/how-many-active -volcanoes-are-there-earth.
3. US Geological Survey, "Which volcanic eruptions were the deadliest?" accessed June 3, 2022, https://www.usgs.gov/faqs/which-volcanic -eruptions-were-deadliest.

8 The Enemy Is Us

1. Some believe a generation is 70 years in length. Others believe one generation is a father, then another generation would be the son, and the grandson would be the third generation. All are correct in their own right.
2. "Development of the World Population Since the Beginning of the Common Era," Statista, accessed June 3, 2022, https://www.statista

.com/statistics/262874/development-of-the-world-population-since-the
-beginning-of-the-common-era.

3. Leonard Ravenhill, *Sodom Had No Bible* (self-published, 2012), 7.

9 WHAT HAPPENS WHEN WE DON'T PRAY?

1. Howard and Geraldine Taylor, *Hudson Taylor's Spiritual Secret* (Chicago, IL: Moody, 2009).
2. C.S. Lewis, *Letters to Malcolm: Chiefly on Prayer* (New York, NY: HarperCollins, 2017), 152.
3. Leonard Ravenhill, *Revival God's Way* (Bloomington, MN: Bethany House Publishers, 1983), 69.
4. Ronnie Floyd, *How to Pray* (Nashville, TN: Word Publishing, 1999), 19.
5. Lewis Drummond, *Eight Keys to Biblical Revival* (Minneapolis, MN: Bethany House Publishers, 1994), 190.
6. Andrew Murray, *The Prayer Life* (Chicago, IL: Moody Publishers), 19.
7. Hamilton Smith, *Extracts from the Writings of Thomas Watson* (Central Bible Truth Depot, 1915), Chapter 12: "Praying," https://www.stempublishing.com/authors/smith/WATSON.html.

10 THE EARTH SHOOK

1. US Geological Survey, "Cool Earthquake Facts," accessed June 4, 2022, https://www.usgs.gov/programs/earthquake-hazards/cool-earthquake-facts.
2. Ibid.
3. R.A. Torrey, "Never a Revival Without Mighty Praying," Bible.org, https://bible.org/seriespage/topical-prayer-revival.
4. Dwight L. Moody, qtd. in Dick Eastman, Foreword to Dr. Yonggi Cho, *Prayer: Key to Revival* (Savage, MN: BroadStreet Publishing Group LLC, 2019).
5. William Reid, qtd. in Jon Bonker, *On The Ministry: Writings And Messages From The Puritans* (self-published, 2014), 74.

11 PRAYER IS A BLOODY BATTLEGROUND

1. David Wilkerson, "Prayer Is a Bloody Battleground," YouTube, https://www.youtube.com/watch?v=hH3QFUF1N4s.
2. Jonathan Falwell, "Prayer: The Greatest Battle," *Decision*, January 1, 2019, https://decisionmagazine.com/prayer-greatest-battle.

12 IT CAN BE A MATTER OF LIFE OR DEATH

1. Kim Owens, *Doorkeepers of Revival* (Shippensburg, PA: Destiny Image Publishers, 2021), 50.
2. Charles Spurgeon, *Only a Prayer-Meeting!* (CrossReach Publications, 2021), 88.
3. James Strong, *Strong's Exhaustive Concordance*, G75, "agōnizomai," https://www.blueletterbible.org/lexicon/g75/kjv/tr/0-1.
4. Bishop Samuel, *Profiles in Prayer*, 16.

13 FINNEY AND FATHER NASH

1. "Charles Grandison Finney," Canton Baptist Temple, accesed June 5, 2022, https://christianhof.org/finney.
2. J. Paul Reno, "Prevailing Prince of Prayer," accessed June 5, 2022, https://www.hopefaithprayer.com/prayernew/prevailing-prince-prayer-daniel-nash
3. Ibid.
4. Ibid.
5. Ibid.
6. Ibid.

14 "ARE Y'ALL POOR?"

1. Chuck Smith, *Effective Prayer Life* (Word For Today, 2000), 1.
2. A.T. Pierson, qtd. in Arthur Wallis, *In the Day of Thy Power* (Fort Washington, PA: CLC Publications, 2010), 112.
3. James R. Rogers and William Rogers, *The Cane Ridge Meeting House* (Cincinnati, OH: Standard Publishing, 1910), 59-60.

15 IT STARTED WITH SIX

1. Dan Herbeck, "Crime Was Rampant and Routine in 19th Century New York City," February 10 1991, https://buffalonews.com/news/crime-was-rampant-and-routine-in-19th-century-new-york-city/article_bee1c130-9005-5c8e-9443-a3188c1bb889.html.
2. Ibid.
3. Ibid.

4. Joel T. Headley, *The Great Riots of New York, 1712 to 1873, Including a Full and Complete Account of the Four Days' Draft Riot of 1863* (New York, NY: E.B. Treat, 1873), 129-131.

5. Edwin G. Burrows and Mike Wallace, *Gotham: A History of New York City to 1898* (New York, NY: Oxford University Press, 1998), 583.

6. James L. Huston, *The Panic of 1857 and the Coming of the Civil War* (Baton Rouge, LA: LSU Press, 1999), 13.

7. Christian History Institute, "The Time for Prayer: The Third Great Awakening," https://christianhistoryinstitute.org/magazine/article/time-for-prayer.

8. "America's Last Nationwide Revival: The Businessmen's Revival of 1857-58," https://www.dayandnight.org/businessmens_revival.

9. Charles G. Finney, *Charles G. Finney: An Autobiography* (Old Tappan, NJ: Oberlin College, 1908), 443.

16 Urgency

1. Paul W. Powell, *The Night Cometh* (Tyler, TX: self-published, 2002), 10.

2. Martyn Lloyd-Jones, *Revival* (Wheaton, IL: Crossway Books, 1987), 163.

17 Mobilized for War

1. Bill Vincent, *The Secret Place of God's Power: Intimacy Brings Power* (Litchfield, IL: Revival Waves of Glory, 2013), 91.

18 Violent Praying

1. Samuel Chadwick, *The Path of Prayer* (Kansas City, MO: Beacon Hill Press, 1931), 68.

2. Duncan Campbell, "Revival in the Hebrides," Revival Library, accessed June 6, 2022, https://www.revival-library.org/revival_histories/evangelical/twentieth_century/hebrides_revival_2.shtml.

3. Ibid.

4. Wesley L. Duewel, "The 1859 Prayer Revival in Wales," accessed June 6, 2022, https://heraldofhiscoming.org/index.php/read-the-herald/past-issues/332-past-issues/1995/jun95/4307-the-1859-prayer-revival-in-wales-6-95.

19 Critical 11 Minutes

1. Smith, *Profiles in Prayer*, 11.

20 The Cinderella of the Church

1. Mary Stewart Relfe, *Cure of All Ills* (Montgomery, AL: League of Prayer, 1988), 111.
2. Ibid.
3. Edward Payson, *Memoir: Select Thoughts and Sermons, Volume 1* (Portland, OR: Hyde, Lord, and Duren, 1846), 244.
4. Steve Strang, "John Kilpatrick: Jezebel Is Stepping Out of Shadows to Oppose Revival, Trump's Re-Election," *Charisma News*, April 8, 2019, https://www.charismanews.com/opinion/75858-john-kilpatrick-jezebel-is-stepping-out-of-shadows-to-oppose-revival-trump-s-re-election.
5. Leonard Ravenhill, *Why Revival Tarries* (Minneapolis, MN: Bethany House, 1987), 19.
6. Ibid., 119.
7. Spurgeon, *Only a Prayer-Meeting!* 158.
8. Ibid., 8.
9. Rick Joyner, *The World Aflame* (Charlotte, NC: MorningStar Publications, 1993), 35.

21 Weeping Between the Porch and the Altar

1. Leonard Ravenhill, qtd. in Simon Ponsonby, *God Is for Us: 52 Readings from Romans* (Oxford, UK: Lion Hudson, 2013), 265.
2. James Strong, *Strong's Exhaustive Concordance*, G2799, "klaio," https://www.blueletterbible.org/lexicon/g2799/kjv/tr/0-1.

22 Fill the Bowl

1. Mary Warburton Booth, qtd. in Ed Strauss, *Why Prayer Makes Sense: In the Bible, in History, in Your Life Today* (Value Books, 2014), 67-68.
2. James Strong, *Strong's Exhaustive Concordance*, G3930, "parechō," https://www.blueletterbible.org/lexicon/g3930/kjv/tr/0-1.
3. Ibid., G1556, "ekdikeō," https://www.blueletterbible.org/lexicon/g1556/kjv/tr/0-1.

4. Ibid., G5056, "telos," https://www.blueletterbible.org/lexicon/g5056/kjv/tr/0-1.

5. Ibid., G5299, "hypōpiazō," https://www.blueletterbible.org/lexicon/g5299/kjv/tr/0-1.

23 FIVE LANES OF PRAYER

1. James Strong, *Strong's Exhaustive Concordance*, G4335, "proseuchē," https://www.blueletterbible.org/lexicon/g4335/kjv/tr/0-1.

2. Ibid., G1162, "deēsis," https://www.blueletterbible.org/lexicon/g1162/kjv/tr/0-1.

3. Ibid., G2169, "eucharistia," https://www.blueletterbible.org/lexicon/g2169/kjv/tr/0-1.

4. Ibid., G155, "aitēma," https://www.blueletterbible.org/lexicon/g155/kjv/tr/0-1.

5. Ibid., H6293, "paga," https://www.blueletterbible.org/lexicon/h6293/kjv/wlc/0-1.

6. Ibid., G5241, "huperentugchano," https://www.blueletterbible.org/lexicon/g5241/kjv/tr/0-1.

24 HOW TO PRAY FOR THE UNSAVED

1. Richard Eby, *Caught Up Into Paradise* (Grand Rapids, MI: Fleming H. Revell Co., 1990), 229-230.

2. "Airplane Crashes," NSC.org, accessed June 8, 2022, https://injuryfacts.nsc.org/home-and-community/safety-topics/airplane-crashes.

ABOUT THE AUTHOR

Todd Smith and his wife Karen have served as the senior pastors of Christ Fellowship Church for 10 years. Along with serving in pastoring roles for over 25 years, Pastor Todd has preached the gospel, led crusades, traveled to the mission fields, and participated in pastors conferences in over 25 countries around the world, as well as hosting the outbreak of the North Georgia Revival that began on February 11, 2018. Pastor Todd and Karen are currently traveling all over the world and spreading revival fire wherever they minister.